Woman, I Am Devotional

*A Woman's Guide to Recognizing
Identity and Fulfilling Purpose*

CHARDONEÉ WRIGHT

WESTBOW
PRESS
A DIVISION OF THOMAS NELSON
& ZONDERVAN

Copyright © 2014 Chardoneé Wright.

All rights reserved. No part of this book may be used or reproduced by any means, graphic, electronic, or mechanical, including photocopying, recording, taping or by any information storage retrieval system without the written permission of the publisher except in the case of brief quotations embodied in critical articles and reviews.

Scriptures taken from the Holy Bible, New International Version®, NIV®. Copyright © 1973, 1978, 1984, 2011 by Biblica, Inc.™ Used by permission of Zondervan. All rights reserved worldwide. www.zondervan.com The "NIV" and "New International Version" are trademarks registered in the United States Patent and Trademark Office by Biblica, Inc.™ All rights reserved.

Scripture quotations are from The Holy Bible, English Standard Version® (ESV®), copyright © 2001 by Crossway, a publishing ministry of Good News Publishers. Used by permission. All rights reserved.

WestBow Press books may be ordered through booksellers or by contacting:

WestBow Press
A Division of Thomas Nelson & Zondervan
1663 Liberty Drive
Bloomington, IN 47403
www.westbowpress.com
1 (866) 928-1240

Because of the dynamic nature of the Internet, any web addresses or links contained in this book may have changed since publication and may no longer be valid. The views expressed in this work are solely those of the author and do not necessarily reflect the views of the publisher, and the publisher hereby disclaims any responsibility for them.

Any people depicted in stock imagery provided by Thinkstock are models, and such images are being used for illustrative purposes only. Certain stock imagery © Thinkstock.

ISBN: 978-1-4908-3073-5 (sc)
ISBN: 978-1-4908-3074-2 (hc)
ISBN: 978-1-4908-3072-8 (e)

Printed in the United States of America.

Library of Congress Control Number: 2014905421

WestBow Press rev. date: 03/20/2014

Dedication

Of course, I thank my heavenly Father, the dad who raised me in His army. I love you, Father, and may my life bear witness to Your wonderful glory. May You be glorified through this book and every work my hands find to do. This book is also dedicated to the beautiful queens of Woman, I Am Incorporated. These wonderful women believed in the vision the Lord gave me and have been nothing but wonderful supporters. Thank you for commitment and dedication to this organization.

Contents

Dedication v
Preface ix
Acknowledgments xi
Introduction xiii

Chapter 1: January
The Lost Rib 1

Chapter 2: February
The Suitable Helper 15

Chapter 3: March
The Purpose-Filled Woman 27

Chapter 4: April
The Woman of High Influence 41

Chapter 5: May
The Compassionate Woman 53

Chapter 6: June
The Patient Woman 65

Chapter 7: July
The Constant Forgiver 77

Chapter 8: August
The Power of Knowledge 87

Chapter 9: September
The Praying Woman 99

Chapter 10: October
The Wise vs. Foolish Woman 111

Chapter 11: November
Insecurity, Fear, and Rejection: Those Hidden Darts 125

Chapter 12: December
The Bold Woman: Stepping out on a Vision 137

About the Author 151
Referenced Works 153

Preface

As the founder of Woman, I Am Incorporated, I am committed to empowering women to make healthy decisions for their lives spiritually, mentally, and physically. The topics of this devotional are a combination of lessons I taught to WIA members and many issues women face daily. This book is divided into twelve sections, one for each month of the year. Each month has a specific focus. This devotional provides scriptural references for meditation and memorization, monthly goals and challenges, prayers to recite, and reflection questions to aid in personal reflection and development. Through this devotional, it is my goal to inspire women to break out of detrimental and negative cycles, to encourage women to develop a solid relationship with Jesus Christ, and to help them recognize their God-given purpose.

For more information about WIA, please visit **www.womaniaminc.com**

Acknowledgments

Thank you to Senior Pastor Mattie Atkinson Darden, Executive Pastor Willa Darden Moody, and my mother, Debora Stanley—all phenomenal women who have helped nourish and water me. A special thanks to my editor, Loren Brown, for her guidance, time, advice, and help in bringing this devotional to life.

Introduction

The *Woman, I Am Devotional* can benefit all women. Whether you long for a deeper walk with God or simply desire guidance, this twelve-month devotional was created for you.

Over the course of a year, this guide will open your heart and mind to the many facets of being a woman. Every month has a specific focus – uniquely designed to encourage and motivate you to walk in the calling that God has for your life.

If only we would begin to dig deeper into the depths of our own soul, we would quickly realize the power and potential that lies within us. It is essential that every woman understand the queen God created her to be. When this revelatory truth permeates the flesh and bleeds into a woman's spirit, her eyes will open to fulfill the call on her life.

January
The Lost Rib

Do you ever feel like a wave of the sea being tossed back and forth? Do you ever feel you are just wandering and drifting aimlessly to and fro without direction, without self-control? Is it so bad that you don't even realize you are being tossed back and forth? Are you trying to fit in with the crowd and do everything everyone else around you is doing? Have you fallen into destructive traps and made horrible decisions based on the control that others may have had over you? Just like a wave … drifting … floating … lost … without direction. You may be that lost rib today. If you are, I have wonderful news: you were destined to read this book. It is my intention to steer you in the right direction, to push you to form an intimate relationship with God and empower you to be the woman God called you to be. For the month of January, I want you to focus on unlocking your self-identity.

Let me start by posing a simple question. Who are you? The only way you will truly understand your identity is to understand God. Your identity is found in Christ alone. It's not found in your bank account, your social status, your job, or in any of your relationships. You have a destiny to fulfill, and there is great potential on the inside of you.

The key to unlocking your destiny is to understand not only your identity but also what you were created to do. If you don't recognize your identity, how will you understand your path in life? Are you the lost rib today, wandering aimlessly, searching for fullness and joy in relationships, money, family, or jobs? Completeness is not found in the mundane aspects of life. It is found and maintained in the Lord.

A Woman's Origin

Who was the first woman on earth? What was she like? What do you have in common with this woman? Where do you really come from? Every woman is created and formed by God and for God. The word *create* means, "to bring something into being; give rise to; make."[1] The word *form* means, "to put into shape, mold, organize; train; shape in the mind."[2]

God brought you into existence (i.e., He created you) by forming your personality, your traits, your gifts, your identity, and your talents. Every part of you was intricately designed and carefully planned. He knows every intimate detail about you—your favorite color, what upsets you, the hidden things you don't discuss. He knows them all. He already knows your thoughts before they come into your mind. You can't hide anything from Him. He knows you better than you know yourself.

---

[1] "Created" *Webster's New Basic Dictionary & Thesaurus*. 2010. Print.
[2] "Form." *Webster's New Basic Dictionary & Thesaurus*. 2010. Print.

God took time to create you. You are not a mistake. You are fearfully and wonderfully made. It is a disgrace and an insult to God when we don't accept ourselves. Maybe you were bullied or teased about your appearance. Maybe someone spoke harsh words to you, and those words cut deep into your soul. Whatever the case, I am here to tell you that you are somebody, and you can make it. You have a destiny and a future. God wants to renew your hope and your expectations in Him. Expect Him to come through for you. Expect Him to deliver you from your struggles. Expect Him to work out every detail of your life. He is with you, even until the end of time.

You Are Made in the Image of God

Every woman was created in the image of God and designed to exercise dominion and authority over the earth. The word *dominion* means "sovereignty and rule."[3] When Jesus Christ bore our sins on the cross and rose again, He gave believers power and authority to rule and reign on this earth. If we have accepted Him as our Savior, Christ's redemptive work has put us in right standing with God.

We never want to be alienated from God. Apart from Him, we can't do anything. We need power to fulfill our destinies. What would it profit us to build ministries, businesses, and so on and have no power? The power that comes from God enables us to walk boldly and to achieve victory over every area of our lives. The power of God

---

[3] "Dominion." *Webster's New Basic Dictionary & Thesaurus*. 2010. Print.

destroys every false burden and strongholds we may carry. God's power can live inside us and allows us to reach our greatest potential.

If we go to the book of Genesis, we see God desired to commune with someone. He fashioned and formed the heavens and the earth first. Then humanity was created to inhabit and cultivate the ground. The first man to walk the earth was Adam. Eve was the first woman created, formed from Adam's rib.

One of the primary reasons humanity came into existence was to worship God. God wants to talk to us, and He loves it when we pray to Him. He wants to show us many wonderful things about our lives. There is higher ground for us to walk. He wants to show us the path and direction our lives should go in. He has already mapped out our lives, but so many times we stray or choose a different path because of disobedience and rebellion.

Why do so many women turn their backs on God? Why do they choose to idolize their boyfriends, husbands, jobs, money, and material possessions to bring them comfort? Oh, women, if we would just learn how to leave our burdens and worries at the feet of Jesus, we would begin to grow in Him. We would begin to see clearly the path on which we should walk if we just took time out for God.

If you only knew the awesome destiny and plan for your life, you would run to meet Jesus every day in prayer. That is my goal—that after reading this book, you will be so motivated that you will make God your everything and the center of your life. There is nothing more beautiful than a woman after God's own heart, neatly tucked in the palm of His hands. You were never designed to be abused, walked on, trampled, or victimized. Do you know how precious you are in His sight? Since you are made in the image of God, you are the exact replica of Him.

Every woman has the potential to be great. You carry seeds of potential in your belly. Over time, those seeds are constantly watered by negative or positive influences. Watered properly, the seed of potential can birth the great plan God has preordained for you. If that seed is negatively influenced, your gifts and talents lie dormant, because you have allowed outside circumstances, lack of communication with God, and/or plain rebellion to cloud the vision of where God wants to take you.

Your true identity will be revealed once you start seeking God. To "seek" means "to make search or enquiry for."[4] I want you to search for and pursue God. Where do you begin? Right where you are, and just as you are. Don't put on a show for God. Come as you are, and talk to Him. Talk to Him every day. In order to hear from God clearly, you must spend time with Him.

A clear indication that you are not spending time with God is if you are irritable, moody, stressed, cranky, and/or depressed. I know this because I have been there. When I failed to spend daily time with God, it was easier for me to become upset and have a short fuse. Yet when I made up in my mind to pour my heart out to God—to

---

[4] "Seek." *Webster's New Basic Dictionary & Thesaurus*. 2010. Print.

sacrifice sleep, and pray—an unspeakable joy and peace filled and ruled over my heart.

I'm not promising problems won't arise in your life, but I am promising that your attitude toward any challenge will change for the better when you have the love of God dripping from inside you. That love is magnified and intensified in your secret place. Every woman must have a "secret place," where she meets to commune, dance, sing, and fellowship with God. It may be your bed, closet, bathroom, car, or favorite chair, but your secret place is where you daily meet with God to talk, cry, scream, kick, worship, and lay it all before Him. You are transformed in that place.

Maybe you aren't provided with the luxury of having your own room or private space, but make a way. Take a daily walk and talk with Him. Commune with Him while you clean your house. There are no limits. God doesn't care about your location or what you look like when you come to Him. Just go! He is more concerned about filling every void in your life and transforming your heart.

Again, if you are that lost rib today, you can come back, and God will welcome you with open arms. He absolutely will not hold your past against you, He wants to guide you through every season of your life. Over the course of January, I want you to make it a daily priority to spend time with God! You know your work and/or school schedule, so designate a time that works for you.

January Goals

1) I challenge you to spend genuine daily time with God. Regulate accountability by partnering with a friend who will help keep you on track. Minimum time: 1 hour

2) Meditate/reflect on the Scriptures below. Every day read and recite Scripture until you have memorized them all.

3) Post encouraging quotes/Scriptures around your room, mirror, in your car so you can visually and consistently see positivity.

Scriptural Reflection

Below are four Scriptures to focus on. You can study one per week for every month. Upon meditation and memorization, study the surrounding text of the passage as well for maximum benefit. I highly suggest purchasing a concordance, study Bible, and Bible dictionary. In addition to the Scriptures listed, I recommend studying and meditating on Genesis chapters 1 and 2.

Week 1: "So God created man in His own image, in the image of God he created him; male and female he created them" (Genesis 1:27 NIV).

- Who said this Scripture (author of the book)?
  _____

- Why was this Scripture said?
  _____
  _____

- What was going on during this time for that caused the Scripture to be said? (Read the surrounding text.)
  _____
  _____

- How does the Scripture apply to your life? What do you personally take from it?
  _____
  _____
  _____

Week 2: "Before I formed you in the womb I knew you, before you were born, I set you apart" (Jeremiah 1:5 NIV).

- Who said this Scripture (author of the book)?

  _____

- God is the master creator. Name a few attributes that you love about yourself.

  _____

  _____

- Does this Scripture indicate that God knows everything about you? How so?

  _____

  _____

- How does the Scripture apply to your life? What do you personally take from it?

  _____

  _____

  _____

  _____

  _____

  _____

  _____

Week 3: "For I know the plans I have for you," declares the Lord, "plans to prosper you and not to harm you, plans to give you hope and a future. Then you will call upon me and come and pray to me and I will listen to you" (Jeremiah 29:11–12 NIV).

- Who said this Scripture (author of the book)?

  _____

- What kind of plans does God have for your life? What is promised to His children?

  _____

  _____

  _____

- How do we get God to listen to us—what must we do?

  _____
  _____

- How does the Scripture apply to your life? What do you personally take from it?

  _____
  _____
  _____
  _____

Week 4: "Glorify the Lord with me; let us exalt His name together. I sought the Lord, and he answered me; he delivered me from all my fears" (Psalm 34:3–4 NIV).

- Who said this Scripture (author of the book)?

  _____

- Look up the definition of "glorify" and "exalt." How can you glorify and exalt God in your life?

  _____
  _____
  _____
  _____

- What did the writer have to do before the Lord answered Him? Are you searching for answers from God concerning your identity? What step must you take in order for God to answer your prayers?

  _____
  _____
  _____
  _____

- Take inventory. What area of your life needs deliverance so that total freedom is attained? What areas do you believe you have been walking blindly in that has deterred you from recognizing your identity in Christ? (Ex.: ungodly relationships, pride, low self-esteem.)

_____
_____
_____
_____
_____
_____
_____
_____
_____
_____
_____
_____
_____
_____
_____
_____
_____
_____
_____
_____
_____
_____
_____
_____
_____
_____

Reflection Questions

1) What has shaped your perception about your origin (school, culture, society, media)?

2) Before reading January's lesson, what perception did you have about your origin?

3) What areas in your life have you have been struggling tremendously with? Ask God to reveal those areas to you, and seek His help. What steps can you take to alleviate their effects on you? For example, if you are struggling with fornication, who in your life is influencing you to have sex? Do certain movies or music enhance those sexual feelings? How can you remove yourself from situations that feed your struggle?

4) What personal changes do you need to implement in your life in order to spend time with God? Do you have to formulate a different sleep schedule, set aside quiet time, turn off your phone, and limit time on the Internet? What has your attention? What is pulling your undivided attention away from God?

Prayer

You can recite this prayer as much as you want. Recite it until you believe it.

> Father, in the name of Jesus, please forgive me for my sins and wipe my slate clean. I thank You for fearfully and wonderfully creating me. I desire to learn my self-identity. Show me who I am in Christ. Show me my worth. Open my eyes to my value. I know I am not a mistake, and I have purpose written all over my life. I desire to live for You and to formulate a better relationship with You through the help of the Holy Spirit. Help me to trust You and learn Your ways. Open my eyes that I may see Your glory. I pray that the eyes of my heart may be enlightened, that I grow in wisdom and stature every day, and that You will free me from every yoke of bondage in my life. I trade my will for Your will, and I say yes to You today, Lord. Show me how to be the woman You have called me to be. Surround me with other godly women who will help lead me in the way that I should go. In Jesus' name, Amen.

February

The Suitable Helper

Congratulations! I hope you have made a consistent effort to spend time with God daily and have memorized the Scriptures from the previous chapter. Don't stop spending time with Him!

Now that you have some information regarding your identity, I want to inform you that your help is needed as a woman. Take a look around your community, your workplace, and your family. Are you able to recognize men and women who need a helping hand? Have you ever tried to reach out to a stranger and help him or her? What better touch does a child receive when they have fallen off their bicycle? What better comfort does a husband receive when he is having a bad day? The touch of a woman is complete with God's gentleness. There is something amazingly beautiful about being a woman. We are to exhibit gentleness in all that we do, because God has uniquely designed and fashioned us to be, "A suitable helper for the world."

Let's go back to Genesis. Here we have Adam and God living the life. Adam is completely whole and content, walking with God and living with purpose. All of Adam's needs are met, and he doesn't want for anything. One day, God looked upon His creation and said, "It is not good for the man to be alone, I will make a helper suitable for him" (Genesis 2:18). Understand that nowhere in the Bible does it declare that Adam asked for a wife. Adam was busy spending time with God, and it was God who saw the need for Adam to receive help.

What is a helper? A helper is someone who contributes to the fulfillment of a need. A helper is an "aide, assistant and supporter."[5] The Lord saw a need in the man and created a woman to fulfill that need. Her name was Eve. You have the DNA of Eve. You are the right and appropriate assistant to somebody. Your destiny is linked to whatever needs you contribute to. A helper makes up in the areas that others lack in. A helper is not a complainer or gossiper but is constantly ready to give a helping hand wherever necessary. To fulfill any need, you must first understand your identity as a woman (chapter 1). Why do you believe women have nurturing and caring characteristics? We are literally born with them. We are ready to help! We are born to help! Help the world. Help your community. Help your family. Help your coworkers wherever necessary. What visions do you have? What are you doing with them? Are you sitting on your talents or actively pursuing them?

Just because you assist others doesn't mean you are of a lower stature than they. Think about it this way. Christ helps us in our daily walk by strengthening us, filling us with joy, and all of the other wonderful blessings he has bestowed on us. Christ does this because He has something we lack and need. Christ helps us. That doesn't mean Christ is to be stepped upon or looked down on just

---

[5] "Helper." *Webster's New Basic Dictionary & Thesaurus.* 2010. Print.

because He helps us. In fact, we should express gratitude for His help. That should be your perspective about helping others. Help out of the kindness of your heart and not because you are looking for a reward. No one should look down on you because you help others. Don't let anyone make you feel inferior to him or her because of your zeal to help. Keep your passion and fire burning. Do you know how many homeless men and women, poverty-stricken neighborhoods, and much more are looking for open shelters, homes, safe houses, businesses, and leaders to help them? You are much needed. Your hands, creativity, touch, and visions are critical to humanity. You are a problem solver. There are problems with your name written all over them. Add your partnership with God, and that's an unstoppable duo! If God is before you, who can be against you? Next time you feel procrastination building up or laziness sneaking its ugly head into your life, remember our suffering human race, waiting for you. You make a difference and are needed.

I don't know what God has called you to do, but it is something powerful, big, and great. I know this because God doesn't create mistakes or mishaps. Before you were born, He divinely ordained and appointed you to live out your purpose. With God, you can go as high as you want. All things are possible to those who believe. There are no limits in God. You never want your gifts and talents to lie dormant out of fear or insecurity. God is with you! What is holding you back? What is your excuse? Do you really trust God with your whole heart? What are you waiting for? Let's get moving! The world doesn't revolve around us; it revolves around God! He wants the glory out of your life. It's time to put behind us all selfish motives. Get rid of them. Stop focusing so much on what you don't have and begin to wholeheartedly be grateful for what you have. Start there, and think about what resources are available to you. Sometimes you just have to think. You came to this world equipped, and it's time to stop sitting on all that potential.

February Goals/Challenge

1) I challenge you to set at least one day per week to helping somebody. Some examples are volunteering at your local homeless shelter or soup kitchen, bringing flowers to the elderly, or cleaning a neighbor's house. Whatever your hands find to do, go help someone. Record your experience here. How did you feel when helping someone else? What lesson(s) have you learned from lending a helping hand?

_____
_____
_____
_____
_____
_____
_____
_____
_____
_____
_____
_____
_____
_____

2) Continue to spend daily time with God.

Scriptural Reflection

Week 1: "So the Lord God caused the man to fall into a deep sleep; and while he was sleeping, he took one of the man's ribs and closed up the place with flesh. Then the Lord God made a woman from the rib he had taken out of the man, and he brought her to the man. The man said, "This is now bone of my bones and flesh of my flesh; she shall be called woman, for she was taken out of man" (Genesis 2:21–23 NIV).

- How did the term "woman" come into manifestation?
  _____

- Who brought the woman to the man? How did man and woman originally become acquainted?
  _____
  _____

- Out of all the organs, why do you think God made woman out of a rib? What help does the rib cage play in the body?
  _____
  _____

- How does the Scripture apply to your life? What do you personally take from it?
  _____
  _____

Week 2: "In the same way, let your light shine before men, that they may see your good deeds and praise your Father in heaven" (Matthew 5:16 NIV).

- What has to shine before men (the world)?

  _____

- What good works are hidden inside you that have yet to come out? What gifts and talents are lying dormant that can be used to glorify your Father in heaven?

  _____
  _____
  _____
  _____
  _____

- What does light do? Why do you believe God referred to your gifts and talents as light?

  _____
  _____
  _____
  _____

- What has to happen before people glorify God in heaven? What role do you play in allowing your light to shine? What is the ultimate goal of God in using your purpose to help someone according to the above Scripture? Who does the glory go back to?

  _____
  _____
  _____
  _____
  _____
  _____
  _____
  _____

Week 3:- "If you can?' said Jesus. 'Everything is possible for him who believes" (Mark 9:23 NIV).

- Why do you believe Jesus started this answer with a question? Was He trying to make a bold statement?

  _____
  _____
  _____

- What is possible for one who believes?

  _____
  _____

- Why do you think Jesus places so much emphasis on how much you believe/your faith?

  _____
  _____
  _____
  _____

- What do you believe God for? What do you have to do for that desire to manifest? Read also Psalm 37:3–5.

  _____
  _____
  _____
  _____

Week 4: "But you are a chosen people, a royal priesthood, a holy nation, a people belonging to God, that you may declare the praises of him who called you out of darkness into his wonderful light" (1 Peter 2:9 NIV).

- What four things does God call you in the above Scripture?

  _____
  _____
  _____

- What are you to proclaim? Why proclaim this?

  _____
  _____
  _____
  _____

- What did God call you out of? What did He call you into?

  _____
  _____
  _____
  _____

- According to the Scripture, who do you belong to? What does it mean to "belong to someone"? How will the world know whom you belong to?

  _____
  _____
  _____
  _____
  _____
  _____
  _____
  _____
  _____
  _____
  _____
  _____

- In what areas of darkness are you walking? What does the light of God need to expose in your life? For example, do you have any unconfessed sins, a deceitful heart, a controlling attitude, manipulation problems? You know that "inner voice" that warns you ahead of time that what you are doing or how you are acting isn't right or appropriate. Whatever it is, repent and ask God to forgive, cleanse, and deliver you from it.

_____
_____
_____
_____
_____
_____
_____
_____
_____
_____
_____

Reflection Questions

1) Outside of your daily routine, where can you provide support and assistance to others?

2) In what areas of your life do you need God to personally help you? Be honest.

Prayer

Father in the name of Jesus. I recognize my God-given duty to be a helper to someone in need. Lord, I can't help others without you first helping me. Shine a light on my heart and thoughts. Since you know all things about me, show me myself. What areas of my life are displeasing to you? Where do I need to make adjustments? As you begin to heal me of past hurt, pain and brokenness, I can effectively help others. I thank you for creating me. I thank you that I have hope today. I thank you that all things are working together for my good. May your unfailing and steadfast love transform me into the woman that I was called to be before the foundation of the world. Father, how can I serve you? How can I serve others? Let your light shine through me. May your glory rest on me. Enable me to be a light that shines in this dark world. Create in me a clean heart and renew a steadfast spirit within me. Carry my baggage. I lay my burdens at your feet. I will trust you from this day forward with unwavering faith. You have begun a good work in me and will complete it. I thank you for my future. I praise your wonderful name and I rest in your promises. In Jesus name I pray, Amen.

March

The Purpose-Filled Woman

When you turn on a light switch, you expect light to illuminate the room; when you turn on your faucet, you expect water to flow through it. Why? Because light and running water are the purposes of those items. Purpose is, "The intention, design and aim of something."[6] It is the reason why something exists. God has an intention for your existence. You have purpose. You are not here by chance or by mistake, and God expects a return on His investment. He invested so much in you. You were strategically born during this generation for a reason. I encourage you to maximize your potential and seek God. Imagine waking up every day and knowing exactly what God requires from you. When you know your purpose, you have direction and guidance. You won't be swayed back and forth by the waves of life, because purpose points you in the right direction.

As a woman of purpose, you have to sacrifice. Yes, bad habits need to be broken in order to make room for God to flow in your life. God wants to flow through you. He wants to talk through you. He wants to use your hands to pray for others; your arms to build businesses, ministries, and facilities; and your mouth to proclaim His glory in all the earth. Do not be ashamed of the gospel of Jesus

---

[6] "Purpose." *Webster's New Basic Dictionary & Thesaurus*. 2010. Print.

Christ. Are you hiding your Christianity? Do your coworkers and friends know you are a Christian? Are you running with lukewarm friends (neither hot nor cold)? It is often said you can tell a lot about a person by the five closest people to him or her. Evaluate your surroundings. Do the women you hang with push you toward God? Do they strengthen you in the Lord? Do they pray for you? If not, you have some decisions to make. Take inventory.

You were designed to build up the kingdom of God on earth. Hence, the Lord's Prayer states, "Let your will be done in earth, as it is in heaven." That means God wants His kingdom established on earth. God's name is proclaimed in heaven, and He wants His name proclaimed on earth. God wants you praying for others and leading them toward Him. There are many lost people in the world who need help.

Imagine not stepping out on your purpose. Those books you are supposed to write, those songs sitting in your belly, those businesses you are supposed to start, those sermons that are waiting to be preached and so much more are sitting inside you. Tap into it. Your self-identity is found in Christ. I guarantee that if you start seeking God and prioritizing Him over every area of your life, you will experience such a thick presence of His glory in your life. How wonderful it is to walk and commune with God every day. How wonderful it is to be able to pour out your heart to someone who genuinely cares for you and wants to see you successful and prosperous wherever you go. God is on your team, your number-one supporter and Creator.

He is the alpha and omega. He is that helper, that comforter, that strengthener, that way maker, and so much more. Let Him be that for you. Allow God to elevate and bring you to places you can't even fathom.

I never thought I would be in the position I am in today. I had my ten-year life plan organized in my mind. But as soon as I gave up my own will for God's will, my plans were demolished, and God's plans were poured into me. Yes, I had to go through pain; yes, I had to have my feathers ruffled; yes, I had to give up bad habits, be purged, say no to a lot, walk away from detrimental relationships, cry, seek God, pray more, fast more, prioritize God, and so much more. To this day, I wouldn't trade it in for anything.

Discipline strengthens you, and when God begins to transform you, endure the changes. You cannot afford to walk into a new season of your life with old baggage that keeps you hindered. Let it go, and let God into your business—wholeheartedly. Increase your faith, and believe God wants to use you. Everyone is not purposed to be on the pulpit, but everyone has a ministry. Your ministry is linked to your purpose. You have problems to solve and needs to be met. As we witnessed in Genesis, God created Adam to inhabit the earth. God saw there was a need for someone to cultivate and work the ground, and Adam was designed to meet that need. What does God need you for? Ask Him. What problems around the world are waiting to be solved by you? There is so much inside you. Your gifts and talents have to be exercised in your life. Don't allow opportunities to pass you by because you are afraid of what other people may say or you feel inadequate. God is with you, and whoever He designs He gives them purpose. Someone is waiting for that very idea that has been locked in your heart to be established. Your purpose is great, and the world needs you!

March Goals/Challenges

1) Pray this over yourself every day. Add to the list!

   A Woman's Positive Affirmation List

   —I am a beautiful, precious and wise woman of God.

   —Today I choose to be at peace. My mind isn't racing and my heart isn't burdened. I am not emotionally led. I stand firm on the word of God.

   —I will make healthy and wise choices today concerning my health, and/or children and family.

   —No weapon formed against me will ever prosper because I belong to God.

   —I will not waste time today. I am a productive woman.

   —I will take time out for myself daily. I will sit in quietness and allow God to speak to my heart.

   —Before I make vital decisions, I will bring my cares and prayers to God.

   —I am stress-free and worry-free. Everything is working out for my good, no matter what the outside circumstance looks like.

   —I will leave a legacy for God's glory. Future generations will know I existed.

   —My identity is found in Jesus Christ. I will use my gifts and talents to walk in my purpose and solve problems.

   —I am a problem solver. There are problems waiting for me to solve.

—I can do all things through Christ, who strengthens me.

—I can do everything I put my mind to do.

—Everyday I grow in wisdom and stature.

—Today my mouth is filled with positive language and wisdom.

—I refuse and will not allow gossip or slander to come from my lips. I will only speak positive words to others and encourage them.

—I am grateful today. Today is a great day to be alive.

—I know my worth. Jesus Christ thought I was worth dying for. Therefore, I will not let anyone talk down to me, or undermine or belittle me.

—I am bold and courageous.

—I am lovable, meek, and humble; I walk with character and integrity.

—I'll keep a smile on my face today.

—I'll do good to others. The fruit of the spirit is being perfected in me.

—Everything I do, I know God is watching, so I take heed to every action.

—I have goals and aspirations that I will accomplish.

—I carry myself with dignity.

—Above all else, I am precious in God's sight; I am the apple of His eye. Therefore, I hold high standards for myself.

2) Continue to spend your daily time with God.

Scriptural References

Week 1: "For I know the plans I have for you," declares the Lord. "Plans to prosper you and not to harm you, plans to give you hope and a future" (Jeremiah 29:11 NIV).

- Do you see yourself in this Scripture? How can you identify with this statement? What kind of plans has God promised you according to this Scripture?

  _____
  _____
  _____
  _____

- Look up the definitions of "hope" and "future." This is what God has promised you. How does that make you feel?

  _____
  _____
  _____
  _____
  _____
  _____

- What are you passionate about? What injustices upset you? Whatever sparks an emotion from you is linked to your purpose. List whatever comes to your mind, and pray over your list.

  _____
  _____
  _____
  _____
  _____
  _____

- God wants to prosper the works of your hands. He wants you to succeed and prosper over everything you set your hands to do. Let's take a look at some more promises. Read Deuteronomy 28:1–14.

Week 2: "Many are the plans in a man's heart, but it is the Lord's purpose that prevails" (Proverbs 19:21 NIV).

- How many plans are in someone's heart?

  _____
  _____
  _____
  _____
  _____
  _____
  _____
  _____

- Whose purpose prevails? Read also Proverbs 16:3. What goals and aspirations do you need to commit to God?

  _____
  _____
  _____
  _____
  _____
  _____
  _____

- According to the Scripture, where does a person's plans begin?

  _____
  _____
  _____

- Read John 6:38. Who sent Jesus to earth? For what reason? (Read a few verses ahead.) Why was Jesus so adamant about doing this? What can you learn from Jesus' obedience? What work/purpose has God called you to be obedient to?

_____
_____
_____
_____
_____
_____
_____
_____

Week 3: "There is a time for everything, and a season for every activity under heaven" (Ecclesiastes 3:1 NIV).

- Why must you wait on God's timing for anything you pray for? What is a consequence of moving ahead of God and listening to your own emotions?

_____
_____
_____

- Was there ever a time in your life when you wished you waited on God's approval before stepping into it? What was it? How might your life be different if you had waited on God?

_____
_____
_____
_____
_____
_____

- Do you feel inadequate at times, exhibit low self-esteem, or have fear of stepping out on God's purpose for your life? Read 2 Timothy 1:7; Matthew 10:31; Psalm 56:3; Isaiah 51:12 for comfort.

- Meditate on Proverbs 4:25-27.

Week 4: "And we know that in all things God works for the good of those who love him, who have been called according to his purpose" (Romans 8:28 NIV).

- Despite any negativity and pain you have endured until now, what does the Scripture tell us God will do with "all these things"?

    _____
    _____
    _____
    _____
    _____

- Take a moment to reflect on your life. What have you overcome? What testimony do you have? Do you truly believe God can use it for your good?

    _____
    _____
    _____
    _____
    _____

- God has called you to purpose for a reason. He has hand-picked you. How can you show gratitude and thankfulness to God?

    _____
    _____
    _____
    _____

- Read Romans 8:31. What confidence can you take from this Scripture? Who fights on your behalf?

Reflection Questions

1) What am I passionate about? What is my inner desire?"

2) What wouldn't I mind doing for the rest of my life, even without a paycheck?

3) What community resources are available that would help me fulfill my purpose?

4) Do you have a journal/notebook where you write down your goals in an organized manner? How can you implement more organization to your life?

5) What comes natural to you?

6) Are you ready for a new season in your life? Pray about your purpose – ask God why you were born!

Prayer

Father in the name of Jesus, I thank you for making me unique and special. Mold me into a woman of purpose. There are gifts and talents you have invested inside of me that I am accountable to use for your glory. Draw those unique gifts out of me and teach me to focus and craft them the way you want to. Order my steps. Activate wisdom so that only wholesome talk and knowledge come from my mouth. I am content with whatever you choose to give me. Keep my lips from gossip and slander. Put a guard over my lips. I will hide your word in my heart so that I may not sin against you. Let my words always be used to edify and build up those around me and not to tear anyone down. Mold me into a Proverbs 31 woman. Help me to practice self control.

Open my eyes to see wonders from you. Help me to submit, surrender and fully obey your statues so that I walk in obedience. Lord, teach me my worth. Let your grace and mercy abound around me as I live day-to-day. Turn my heart towards you and take out anything that is not like you. Examine my motives daily. You said in your word that the pure in heart shall see you. Therefore, purify my heart and hands. I understand I am called to greatness. Therefore, surround me with men and women after your heart.

Take away all distractions and knock the taste out of my mouth for the things of this world. Help me to focus on You.

Teach me how to live a consecrated life all for your glory. You gave believers the awesome inheritance of dominion and power. Therefore, I exercise my authority over this earth with full confidence that my prayers shall reach your ears. You said that whatever I confess with my mouth and believe in my heart, I shall have. So I confess that from this day forward, I will be a woman after your own heart and I choose to live a life that is pleasing to you and not humans. I believe in my heart that you have great and mighty things in store for me. I intend to accomplish every work I set my hands to do. Thank you for all you do in my life and will continue to do. May I always be grateful. I ask all of this in Jesus name. Amen

April

The Woman of High Influence

When Satan wanted to cause Adam to fall into sin, he tempted His wife, Eve. She had influence over her husband. You have influence—positive or negative—over others. How do you use that influence? Women are influential on the job, in their families, in marriage, in church, and everywhere their feet go. Our influence determines so much. Remember that someone is always watching you. They are watching to see if what you speak lines up with your actions. Are your actions contradicting your words? Are you saying one thing but doing another? How can someone trust you if they can't trust your word?

Women ought to bring peace to every situation around them. You are a peace carrier; peace should radiate through you at all times. Be that comforting and compassionate woman who optimistically finds the good in everyone. In these toxic and evil times, the world thirsts for women of great influence to stand up for biblical standards and holy living. Remember, you have to give an account to God for the way you live. Don't manipulate or use your power to control others. Use your influence positively. Make a difference in someone's life.

As a mother, your children are always watching. They watch how you handle situations. Your daughters will emulate the example you set, and your sons will learn how to treat women based on your influence. Whatever influence you exhibit will set the course for the legacy you leave. When you are gone from this earth, how will people know you lived? What footprints will you leave? How do you want to be remembered?

Similarly, a wife is the helper to her husband; she's the backbone he needs. When you are married, you have the opportunity to speak life into your husband every day. God wants you to push your husband toward his purpose and to do him good all the days of your life. Your influence as a wife is tremendous. Every husband wants to be honored. They want to know their wife respects his position as the spiritual leader and priest of the home. Don't tear him down with your words or belittle him. Appreciate your king. Show kindness toward his needs. How can you encourage him? How can you lift him up and motivate him to be the man of God he was called to be?

When husband and wife are in alignment with the roles God designed, God has the opportunity to flow freely through that marriage. God doesn't flow in disorder and chaos. If you want a successful marriage, understand your role as a wife of high influence. Understand his role as the leader of the home, and seek God for wisdom and direction in meeting those needs. Then use that positive influence to fuel your husband and marriage. God has to be the center of your life for you to properly function in your role as a wife.

Lastly, as a leader in any business/ministry/workplace, your morals and ethics characterize your behavior. Be a woman of integrity—the same in the dark and in the light. As a leader in the workplace, your word is your bond. When you make promises, keep them. Always take your concerns and questions to God in prayer for direction concerning the path you should take. As a leader, evaluate the gifts and talents your team possesses, and cultivate that for the betterment of your company or business endeavor. Speaking to the seeds of greatness inside of others will stir and revive their spirits.

Everyone came to this planet equipped with gifts and talents, but everyone isn't afforded the opportunity to express those gifts. So open doors for others, and speak life to them daily. Ask God to open your eyes for opportunities to bless others. Eyes will always be on you, so use these opportunities to show the love of God through every task. There should be something different about you—in the way you walk, the way you talk, and how you handle situations. A woman of high influence isn't easily swayed by the opinions of others but, rather, confidently trusts in the living God. Every area of your life has to be turned over to God. Keeping Him first is vital in making healthy choices for your family and personal well-being.

April Goals/Challenges:

1) Write a list of the top five people you spend the most time with. Think about what kind of influence your life brings to them? Evaluate your circle. Do you need to make any changes? Are you constantly the only positive one in the bunch? Do these women pray or gossip with you? Do they push you closer to God or away from Him?

2) Research an already established organization/charity/support group in your local city that needs help. How can you use your gifts and talents to sow/help their ministry? How can you become a positive influence for their organization?

3) Remember your "secret place" never gets put on the back burner. Keep spending that daily time with God.

Scriptural References

Week 1: "Don't let anyone look down on you because you are young, but set an example for the believers in speech, in life, in love, in faith and in purity" (1 Timothy 4:12 NIV).

- In what five ways are you to set an example for other believers? Do you struggle being a positive influence in any of these areas? What daily changes can you implement for transformation to occur?

- The above Scripture comforts young believers. Has anyone ever looked down on you or tried to intimidate you because you were younger than him or her? What was your response? If you are approached with that same situation, will you handle it differently? How?

- Was there ever a time in your life when you've spoken negative words or slandered someone else? Repent of this. Going forward, how can you use your speech to edify others?

- How can you personally set an example for others through love? Is there anything hindering you from expressing love toward others? Are there any damaged areas of your life that won't allow you to express love?

Week 2: "You are the salt of the earth. But if the salt loses its saltiness, how can it be made salty again? It is no longer good for anything, except to be thrown out and trampled by men" (Matthew 5:13 NIV).

- What is the purpose of salt? What are you the "salt" of? What is Jesus referring to here?

- How can you keep yourself free from the ways of the world but still flavorful for God to use? Are there any distractions in your life that keep you from fully obeying God? How can you get rid of these distractions?

  _____
  _____
  _____
  _____
  _____
  _____
  _____

- Meditate on Mark 9:50.

Week 3: "I can do everything through him who gives me strength" (Philippians 4:13 NIV).

- How many things can you do through Christ?

  _____
  _____

- Where does your strength come from? How can you receive this strength from God? Have you been burdened lately by trying to carry the load yourself?

  _____
  _____
  _____
  _____
  _____
  _____
  _____
  _____

- Define the word *through*. How does it pertain to you and Christ? Is there anything you are holding in your heart that disables Christ's ability to work through you? How can you rid yourself of this encumbrance?

  _____
  _____
  _____
  _____
  _____
  _____

- What must you do to remain content in all circumstances, regardless of life's tribulations and trials? How can you remain a positive influence in the midst of any storm?

  _____
  _____
  _____
  _____

Week 4: "She watches over the affairs of her household and does not eat the bread of idleness" (Proverbs 31:27 NIV).

- How can you watch over the affairs of your household? How are you influencing those in your household?

  _____
  _____
  _____

- Define "idleness." Have you been eating its fruit? In what areas of your life has procrastination reared its ugly head? How can you change that starting today?

- What have you been putting off that you know God has called you to do (writing books, songs, stepping out on a business idea)? If this is you, what is the root of your procrastination? What is hindering you from taking that next step? Remember, someone needs you.

- Was there ever a time in your life when you were a negative influence on someone? What was the consequence?

Reflection Questions

1) How will others know about your contributions to the world? What legacy would you like to leave?

2) Who is your role model? Why did you choose this person? What kind of influence has this person had on you? How can you exhibit this same influence over others?

3) Have you ever felt worthless? Have you ever felt inadequate? Talk to God about these feelings. No matter what you have done in your past, God can heal you and use you as an influential woman!

4) Whether you are single, married, or courting, what underlying characteristics should a virtuous, high-influencing woman practice daily?

Prayer

Father, in the name of Jesus, I desire to be a woman of great influence. I know my life will leave a legacy, but I need Your constant help and support along the way.

Bring me around men and women who can act as accountability partners with me and pray for me. Lord, bring full restoration to every broken and hurt area of my life. I desire to be whole, so Your plans and purposes are manifested in my life. Show me how to be a positive influence around my family and friends.

Lord, show me the way. I am nothing without You. I am lost without Your guidance, and I delight in loving Your righteous decrees and commands. Restore my purity if I have allowed the world to pollute and contaminate my soul and spirit. Today I decree and declare that I am being transformed into the woman God has created me to be. Father, I ask You to open up doors for me that no one can shut. Fill me with your presence. I embrace my future today. In Jesus name I pray. Amen.

May

The Compassionate Woman

Although we all are unique individuals, when you think about it, what really makes you different from your neighbor? Is it the color of their skin, their culture, heritage, or religion? In essence, we all come from God but born into different families. We are all brothers and sisters. We all have the same father if we accept salvation. Why is it that some of society is looked down on because of their appearance? You have no clue who God will raise someone up to be, so we must be careful of how we treat others. If only our hearts were filled with more compassion. If only we chose to love others rather than gossip or slander their name and reputation. If only we chose to lift our brothers and sisters in prayer when we see them struggling, rather than tear them down with our mouths.

When was the last time you did a compassionate deed for someone else? When was the last time you went out of your way to bless someone less fortunate than you? Show appreciation, and express sympathy, empathy, concern, and consideration for the needs of others. I guarantee any gesture, no matter how small, has the ability to make someone's day. You have no clue what people go through, and simply showing compassion toward them makes a difference.

Make a difference in someone's life today. I remember praying to God and simply asking for more compassion to fill my heart. I wanted to see the world through Christ's eyes. I wanted to look at situations the way Christ did. I wanted to look beyond people's faults and see the real them. When I look at people affected by poverty, homelessness, and other detrimental challenges that plague the world, I try to imagine myself in their shoes. You know what I mean—that prostitute you may have joked or laughed at; the homeless man sitting at the street corner, begging for change; or even that guy or girl covered in tattoos and piercings who everyone stares and points at. Yes, God loves them as well. He loves us all equally.

If only we begin to understand the compassion that fills the heart of Christ. He is so compassionate and loving toward us. As you begin to seek Him, that love will fill you up. Then you must pour out that same love everywhere you go. Smile. Encourage someone. Motivate your neighbor. Be a blessing.

The greatest bondage every human needs to be saved from is sin. It is what alienates and separates us from God. No matter how mighty some of us may think we are, no human has ever or will ever have the capacity to save himself or herself from sin. When you choose to turn your back on God, you begin to walk in full darkness. Yes, you wake up every day with breath in your body, but spiritually, you're dead. Before salvation was offered through Christ's redemptive work on the cross, sinners were entangled in many yokes of bondage, walking blind, deceived by the Enemy, and living in divine ignorance because of hardened hearts, filthy and unremorseful personal, sinful behavior. Despite the filth we so carelessly drenched ourselves in, God had pity and compassion on humanity and saw fit to send us help—Jesus Christ.

Just as Jesus was sent to help us, God has preordained you to help others. If the love of God is poured into your heart, you ought to pour that same love and compassion into others. Someone needs your compassion. Someone around you needs Jesus. People are dying every day and going straight to hell because they have been deceived by the Enemy and chose to rebel against God. A wise word from you into the ears of a hopeless person can literally change his or her entire life. Do not be ashamed of the gospel of Jesus Christ.

What has God done for you? What dark pits has He brought you out of? Testify. Be the woman who advances the kingdom of God through her divinely ordained purpose. Be that woman whose compassion and loving heart opens her arms to the poor and needy and serves humanity. What are you waiting for? Everything you need, you already have. You came into this world equipped with seeds of greatness planted inside you. Look inside yourself, and begin to see the beautiful creation God created. Take inventory of your resources and contacts. Who do you know? Think back. Who can you help with what has been given to you? You are a woman, and we have the inner creative ability to work with what we have. If you are a disciple of Christ, you are foremost a servant. Countless times in the Bible we read about Christ's compassion toward others, even toward

His enemies. What a great example to follow. What a great man. He literally paved the way for us to follow. He lived what He preached.

May Goals/Challenge

This month focus on spreading compassion and love everywhere you go. Focus on the needs of others, and take your eyes off whatever it is you are going through. God already knows what you are facing before it hit your life. His arms are strong enough to carry the load, so you need not worry. Just believe and keep praying. Keep serving others. Keep seeking God diligently and wholeheartedly. He rewards those who diligently seek Him. If you want to find the greatest joy on earth, extend a helping hand to someone in need.

Scriptural References

Week 1: "When he saw the crowds, he had compassion on them, because they were harassed and helpless, like sheep without a shepherd. Then he said to his disciples, "The harvest is plentiful but the workers are few" (Matthew 9:36–37 NIV).

- Why did Jesus have compassion for the people? What did He compare them to? What causes you to have compassion for others?

  _____
  _____
  _____
  _____

- What is the job of a shepherd? How does that tie in with Jesus' comparison of the crowd? Do you know anyone like this—helpless?

  _____
  _____
  _____
  _____

- The harvest of people who need Christ is plentiful, but the workers are few. Why do you think this is so? Why do you believe people shy away from working for Christ? In any capacity, can you relate to the above Scripture?

  _____
  _____
  _____
  _____
  _____
  _____
  _____
  _____

- How does being compassionate make a difference in your attitude and behavior personally and professionally?

  _____
  _____
  _____
  _____
  _____

Week 2: "For it is God who works in you to will and to act according to his good purpose" (Philippians 2:13 NIV).

- Who works in you?

  _____

- How can God work through you to accomplish His good purpose?

  _____
  _____
  _____

- Read Philippians 2:14-15. How should you do everything? According to this Scripture, what kind of generation are we living in? What kind of influence would a compassionate woman of God have on this type of generation?

  _____
  _____
  _____
  _____
  _____

- The Bible has many stories of men and women who allowed God to use them for His good purpose. Pick a Bible character and read his or her life story. What obstacles and challenges did the person overcome, even while God was working through the character? How did your character show compassion toward others to fulfill his or her God-ordained assignments?

Week 3: "If anyone has material possessions and sees his brother in need but has no pity on him, how can the love of God be in him?" (1 John 3:17 NIV)?

- Has there been a time when you saw a brother/sister/friend in need and you could have helped but didn't? What does the Scripture say about this attitude/behavior?

- Are you willing to go out of your way for someone else, even if it is inconvenient for you? Do you give room for God to interrupt your plans?

  _____
  _____
  _____

- Examine your heart. Are there any selfish ways God needs to cleanse from you? Do you put others before yourself? Do you bless others? Are you kindhearted? If not, ask Him to take selfishness out of your heart and to fill it with compassion for people and the things of God.

  _____
  _____
  _____
  _____

- What kind of world would exist if everyone exhibited compassion in his or her daily activities? What does compassion bring to such a dark place?

  _____
  _____
  _____
  _____
  _____

Week 4: "For God so loved the world that He gave his one and only Son, that whoever believes in Him shall not perish but have eternal life" (John 3:16 NIV).

- Who did God love so much, and what did He give to them?

  _____
  _____
  _____

- Whoever believes in Jesus has what?

- Can you imagine giving up your only child as a blood sacrifice to atone for sin? Can you imagine the compassion and love God had to feel to give up the very child He loved so dearly? How would you feel if you had to give your child up as a sacrifice?

Reflection Questions

1) Define the word *compassionate*. Are there areas in your life where you could show more compassion toward others? Are you quick to have a nasty attitude when things don't go your way or you are given a task you don't want to do?

2) Do you judge others?

3) Do you criticize others?

Prayer

Father, in the name of Jesus, I thank You for molding me into a compassionate woman. May the compassion and zeal that fills the heart of Christ be poured into my heart in great abundance. Father, show me my own faults, any selfish ways and areas of my life where I haven't been compassionate toward others. I desire to walk in love every day. I desire to love wholeheartedly and to do unto others as I would like them to do unto me. I pray that my compassionate heart serves as a light in such a dark world and that it brings all glory and honor to You. Lord, fill my cup. Help me to respond kindly to everyone. Teach me self-control. If my heart is hardened, make it soft. Help me to cultivate kindness and gentleness through your precious Holy Spirit. In Jesus name I pray. Amen.

June

The Patient Woman

Ever felt like circumstance after circumstance continues to pile up before your eyes? Maybe you've cried. Maybe you've taken your discouragement out on others, or maybe you have just shut down, because you don't want to talk about your situation. The irritation of pain and discouragement can feel like a constant downward spiral. Maybe you have prayed this prayer: "God, I love You and trust You. Why am I having such a hard time? Do You hear my prayers? When will this season of my life pass by? I trust God, and I love You, but why am I going through so much? I'm ready to move forward in my life, but I feel stuck in the same cycle."

Does that sound like you? Why do we have problems? Why can't life just run smoothly? The answer is because God wants to develop perseverance in us. He allows perseverance to finish its work so that you are mature and complete, not lacking anything (James1:1–4). Be steadfast and patient as you go through the trials of life. What does complaining about them do? It only magnifies the problem. Change your perspective on whatever challenges you face today. Use them as opportunities to grow and develop.

How long will you be a baby in Christ? At some time you must transition from spiritual milk to meat. Your reward is at the end, so we must keep a heavenly perspective. God has promised believers so many blessings if they persevere under trials, stand the test, and continue loving God. He knew what you were going to face before it happened. All He wants is your trust. We are to exemplify self-control and patience as we endure these tests and trials. It hurts, but think about your reward from God as you sail through the storms and come out stronger than ever. Sometimes problems draw you closer to God. You learn to trust and rely on Him. You begin to read your Bible more, pray more, and seek Him more. Good can come out of hardships. Stop worrying and stressing out about certain seasons in your life, God allows those doors to open when the time is right. He knows your desires; He put them there. Trust His timing, and focus on your purpose. Everything else will come into alignment.

Trials and testing hurt. They will make you cry, scream, discourage you, and all of the above—if you allow it. Don't fight this season in your life. God is working on you patiently. He is weaning away all the bad. It costs to be a disciple of Christ. Salvation is free, but you have to pay a price to follow God, and it won't always be easy. Yet those who hope in the Lord shall renew their strength. Look to God, which is where your help comes from. The strength and hope you need are found right in His hands. He wants you to lay your burdens at His feet, so He can carry them for you. All you need to do is remain relaxed and calm. Do not panic! This is only a test. You'll pass with flying colors if you remain in God. Don't allow trials to distance you from Him, stop your praise, or hinder your prayers. In fact, that is what the Enemy desires. He wants to silence you. This is the time to give God your best praise and worship. So as you go from day to day, just stop and remember you are blessed, and there is a heavenly Father who cares so much about you that He willingly takes your hand through every storm and walks besides you.

June Goal/Challenges

1) Do you have patience? Do you need to work on developing patience? Write down one to three steps to implement whenever you feel yourself losing patience. These steps should help calm you before any retaliation or before making irrational and emotionally based decisions.

Step 1
_____
_____

Step 2
_____
_____

Step 3
_____
_____

Scriptural References

Week 1: "Do not be anxious about anything, but in everything, by prayer and petition, with thanksgiving, present your requests to God. And the peace of God, which transcends all understanding, will guard your hearts and your minds in Christ Jesus" (Philippians 4:6–7 NIV).

- In what areas of your life do you need peace? After listing these areas, command peace to rule over them. Remember, the believer has been given all power and authority through Jesus Christ. We have commanding power and the ability to speak to our circumstances, and they have to obey.

- Are there people in your life who increase your stress level and decrease your peace of mind? How can you still show the love of God to them while guarding your heart? Do you need to implement boundaries?

- Referencing the above Scripture, what do you have to do before the peace of God can guard your heart and mind in Christ Jesus? Perhaps the peace of God hasn't guarded your heart and mind, because you haven't done this step first.

    _____
    _____
    _____
    _____
    _____
    _____

- What prayers, petitions, and requests do you need to release to God today? After writing them, pray over them.

    _____
    _____
    _____
    _____
    _____
    _____

Week 2: "Peace, I leave with you; my peace I give you. I do not give to you as the world gives. Do not let your hearts be troubled and do not be afraid" (John 14:27 NIV).

- What did Jesus leave you with?

    _____
    _____
    _____

- Is anything troubling your heart today? What does Jesus tell you to do concerning your troubles?

  _____
  _____
  _____
  _____
  _____

- What benefit do you have from receiving what Jesus offers you rather than what the world has to offer? Whose way is better?

  _____
  _____
  _____
  _____

- What overall promises can you rest in today that Jesus has promised for your life? Choose to mediate on these promises rather than on your present circumstances.

  _____
  _____
  _____
  _____
  _____
  _____

Week 3: "Be joyful in hope, patient in affliction, faithful in prayer" (Romans 12:12 NIV).

- Whenever we are afflicted, how are we to respond to this matter?

  _____
  _____

- Define "hope." What kind of hope should you have? Where does this hope come from?

  _____
  _____
  _____
  _____

- What did Christ do when He was constantly rejected by others and eventually crucified? Was He patient? Did He fight back? Did He remain faithful in prayer? Look to Christ as the perfect role model. Emulate His actions. Write one example of Christ displaying a peace of mind and patience in amid chaos.

  _____
  _____
  _____
  _____
  _____

Week 4: "Blessed is the man who perseveres under trial, because when he has stood the test, he will receive the crown of life that God has promised to those who love him" (James 1:12 NIV).

- Define the words *blessed* and *persevere*. When you are in the midst of a storm or rough season in your life, how should you respond to it?

  _____
  _____
  _____
  _____

- What will every believer who has persevered under trial receive from God?

- Why is it important to love God wholeheartedly?

- Why do you believe God tests His children? What good comes from testing? When God tests your patience, how do you respond? What can you do differently?

Reflection Questions

1) What causes you to lose your patience quickly? When that situation arises again, how can you respond differently?

2) How can cultivating patience benefit you?

3) Are you anxious about anything right now? Where do you believe this stems from; what is the root cause? To counteract an anxious heart, meditate and memorize Philippians 4:6–7. Decree and declare this Scripture over your life whenever you feel yourself beginning to lose patience.

Prayer

Never pray for patience or for God to humble you. It is not scriptural. You already have the capacity to cultivate patience and humility with the Holy Spirit's help. Here is a prayer to help aid you in this area.

Father, in the name of Jesus, I repent for being impatient at any time of my life. I desire to lay every care at Your feet today. I know in my heart that You care for me with an everlasting love, and You are ready to meet my needs. Today I ask you to help me practice and exercise self-control in my life. I speak peace to every ounce of anxiousness, stress, anxiety, depression, and oppression my spirit may carry. I decree and declare Philippians 4:6–7 over my life that I am not anxious about anything, but in everything, I present my requests and petitions to You. It is only after I lay these burdens and worries at Your feet that the peace of God, which passes all understanding, is able to guard my heart and my mind in Christ Jesus.

Thank You that I don't have to live with a troubled or fearful heart. I trust Your timing for every season in my life. I understand that whatever You want me to have, You will make provision for it in my life in the correct timing. I choose to focus on You and how blessed I am, rather than what I don't have.

Thank You, God, for being a refuge and a shield of strength for me this day. I thank You for self-control and a peace of mind. Amen.

July

The Constant Forgiver

As I chugged down a gallon of ice cream and watched *Waiting to Exhale,* I remembered thinking, *How did I get here and how do I get up from this place?* Ever had an aha moment, when you sit back and reflect on life? I was about nineteen years old and had recently experienced a bad breakup. I was so overwhelmed with emotions that it blocked and clouded all the logical thinking I had. I didn't eat right and fell into the "victim mentality." I wallowed and cried in pity parties for months, until I was able to gain strength to keep pressing on. How many times has someone hurt you, discouraged you, or upset you? These hurts cut deep into your heart! When we place more trust in humans than in God, we set ourselves up for disappointment. Why put our trust in mere humans who have but a breath in their nostrils (Isaiah 2:22)? All the warning signs were there to tell me of the destruction to come, but I was deceived. I was walking in flesh and put way too much confidence in this flesh rather than God. Eventually, heartbreak and disappointment came knocking full force at my door, ready to take me captive!

Whether someone from your family, a spouse, a coworker, or from a close trusted friend has ever hurt you in any manner, you owe it to yourself to release them. You owe it to yourself to let go of the hurt and pain that filters as a poison to your soul. Unforgiveness can destroy you if it is not taken care of. It's not worth it. Vengeance is of the Lord, and He will repay. You don't have to take matters into your own hands. Choose to pour your heart out to God continually to release those toxic memories.

Forgiveness is releasing any person who has harmed or hurt you. Forgiveness is not for them, but for you! First, pray and ask God to help you forgive them. Pour your heart out to God, and tell Him all about it, how you feel about it, and so on. Tell Him you are making the effort to forgive that person. Then, as hard as it may seem at first, pray for your offender. Ask God to help him or her. If the person caused you hurt, he or she needs help, too. God will honor you, because you made the decision to forgive. Jesus Christ died so God can forgive our sins. Think about how many times you did wrong in the sight of God, how many times you have let God down, how many times you have displeased God. But God welcomes you back with open arms every time you ask Him to forgive you. And in the same manner, you ought to show that for someone else. Forgive as God forgives you. If you harbor grudges toward people, you are drinking poison and only harming yourself. God won't even hear your prayers if there is unforgiveness in your heart. Forgiving someone doesn't mean the pain goes away overnight, but it is the first step in acknowledging and welcoming God into your situation. Once you release it to Him, don't take it back. God saw how they wronged you, and you need not repay or fight back. God will make sure they reap what they have sown. So rest in His arms today, knowing He is pleased you will give this matter to Him.

Notice the title of this chapter is "The Constant Forgiver." Forgive constantly. Forgive daily. Forgive as if your life depended on it. Develop a healthy habit of forgiving. Women, we are that rock in the family. We exemplify strength for our marriage and family. Where in your heart do you have room to harbor ill feelings? Where in your heart do you have room to gossip and slander others? Stop running to your friends every time you have a problem, and start running to the feet of Jesus. He is the only one who can help you the way your soul needs to be comforted. Our mind has the ability to magnify and replay occurrences over and over. If you aren't careful, detrimental circumstances can starve your positive thoughts. You have to feed your faith, or it will starve. Just as you would feed a baby the necessary nutrients and food to grow, you have to feed your inner woman. She needs the vitamins and nutrients of praise, worship, prayer, and the Word of God to properly function. When you are easily irritated, discouraged, and frustrated, those are signs you aren't spending enough time with God. It's time to tune out the voices of those around you, and examine your own heart. Any unconfessed sins lodged behind that smile? Any ill feelings toward your fellow neighbor? Start running to those Scriptures that deal with your circumstance. Pray more and gossip less. Take your pain to God. Take your hurt to God. Tell God all about it. You are so precious to Him and He wants to release your heart of any unforgiveness. Healing takes time, but God promises to stay close to you. You are a reflection and representative of Jesus Christ. If Jesus walks in constant forgiveness, so should you. Never ever forget to forgive, just as you expect Christ to forgive you of any wrongdoing. Have mercy.

July Goals/Challenges

1) Continue to spend daily time with God

2) Make a list of people you need to forgive and why. Bring that list up to the Lord, and ask God to help you forgive everyone on that list who has offended or hurt you in any way. Pour your heart out to God concerning the matter, and allow God to saturate you with a peace about it. Don't spend another day entangled in the yoke of bondage of unforgiveness or dwelling on things of the past. Decide today to let go of that poison. Be free!

3) When you decide to forgive someone who has hurt you, celebrate your healing! It won't happen over night, but it is the beginning of your breakthrough. Take yourself out to a movie, treat yourself to dinner and celebrate your new release. You owe it to yourself.

Scriptural Reference

Week 1: "For if you forgive men when they sin against you, your heavenly Father will also forgive you. But if you do not forgive men their sins, your Father will not forgive your sins" (Matthew 6:14–15 NIV).

- Why do you have to forgive others of their trespasses against you? What happens if you don't forgive others? Is it worth it to hold a grudge?

- Who do you need to forgive today and why, no matter what they have done to you?

- What did it feel like when someone wronged, persecuted, or hurt you for any reason? How do you think God feels when we do the same?

Woman, I Am Devotional

- Read Ephesians 4:32. What kind of attitude should all Christians have toward forgiveness?

Week 2: "But I tell you: Love your enemies and pray for those who persecute you" (Matthew 5:44 NIV).

- If someone hates you, curses you, spitefully uses you, or persecutes you, what does God tell you to do?

- Why do you think God wants you to show love and compassion, even when you were the one who was hurt?

- In forgiving others, what does God teach you?

- Out of all people, why would God tell us to love our enemies? How can you benefit from showing love and positivity to someone who despises you? Who is the bigger person?

　　_____
　　_____
　　_____
　　_____
　　_____
　　_____
　　_____
　　_____

Week 3: "Bear with each other and forgive whatever grievances you may have against one another. Forgive as the Lord forgave you" (Colossians 3:13 NIV).

- What does it mean to "bear with someone"?

　　_____
　　_____
　　_____

- Whose attitude should we emulate when forgiving others? Why?

　　_____
　　_____
　　_____

- Is there anyone you have a complaint against?

　　_____
　　_____
　　_____

- Has it been difficult for you to forgive some people over others? Why do you believe this is so? What burdens can you lay at the feet of Christ today concerning any unforgiveness or bitterness in your heart?

_____
_____
_____
_____
_____

Week 4: "Get rid of all bitterness, rage and anger, brawling and slander, along with every form of malice. Be kind and compassionate to one another, forgiving each other, just as in Christ God forgave you" (Ephesians 4:31–32 NIV).

- What six things should you put away? Define each one.

_____
_____
_____
_____

- Are you carrying around any bitterness or anger in your heart? Why? What and/or whom do you need to release today that has caused bitterness or anger in your heart? Let's get to the root of the problem. Pour your heart out to God concerning this matter, and ask Him to create a clean heart and a renewed, steadfast spirit within you.

_____
_____
_____
_____
_____
_____

- How does this Scripture apply to your life? What do you take personally from it? What part of the Scripture has touched your heart the most?

August
The Power of Knowledge

When I was younger, I would browse encyclopedias for fun. Yes, I was what you called a "nerd," and I loved every bit of it. Growing up, I was always involved in the band, school play, or writing-enrichment programs, because I had a love for creative arts. Isn't it amazing that by exposing yourself to different outlets, you can develop a passion you didn't even know was there? I encourage you to be ambitious. Get out of your normal routine and try something new. It can range from trying a new dish to visiting a new museum.

God created this beautiful earth with such intricate detail. God's creativity reminds me of an artist and his paintbrush. This earth lay bare before His eyes, like an artist lays out a blank piece of paper on an easel. With a stroke of his paintbrush, God colored the world in rich greens, blues, reds, deep yellows, and all other colors. He drew the ocean, land, beaches, trees, flowers, animals, the stars, the sun, the moon and everything in the universe. It is truly remarkable to fathom.

What goes on in the mind of God? His ways are above our ways, and His thoughts are above our thoughts. Everything that was created was first a thought in God's mind. It was manifested after He spoke it into existence. How amazing is it to know the same creative DNA our Father carries lies within us. When you look at a skyscraper, you understand that an architect had to first visualize it in his mind, draw it out on paper, create a model, and then proceed to build. It is the same with God. He dreams of remarkable purposes for our lives and strategically plants those seeds of greatness inside us with the ability to create. Then we are birthed in human form and walk this earth with visions in our bellies. Those visions wait to be birthed at the appointed time.

Once God reveals to you your purpose, there is work to be done. I pray you are revived today if your spirit lacks life. Consider the magnitude of the entire world and know that you were not designed to stay confined in the four walls of your home. Experience something new and refreshing. Read different publications to broaden your view. Research. I believe every woman should be able to have an intellectual conversation about the world's affairs and news. Pay attention to what is going on around you. Spend some time in the library, reading about subjects that interest you. Expose yourself to other cultures. Gain knowledge on a topic that you don't know anything about. We don't live in a box, and there is so much to learn and read about. You must have knowledge about what is happening outside your city's parameters. Knowledge adds to you. Knowledge is truly powerful. Knowledge empowers you. Knowledge opens the doorway of opportunity for you. No one can take away your education or knowledge, so continue to feed it. You can never learn too much. Visit a place you have never been. Become an expert on a certain topic. Find out what interests you, and develop study habits. Soak in all the knowledge you can.

Health Knowledge

You have the power to gain knowledge to make healthy decisions for your life. Don't ever let anyone make you feel you are inadequate, incompetent, or unable to live your purpose. Your uniqueness is what makes you different. The Bible says there is no flaw in you whatsoever (Song of Song 4:7). Who told you that you had flaws? Who are you comparing yourself to? Does your perspective of beauty line up with the Word of God or with society? When you're confident from the inside, it will show on the outside. You have to walk and talk in confidence, knowing you are a child of the most high King. You are beautiful because God is your Father, and He is the Creator of the entire world. It is truly an insult when we don't accept ourselves for who God has designed us to be.

By all means, take care of yourself physically, spiritually, and mentally. A healthy diet, adequate exercise, rest, devotional time with God, and leisure time have to be balanced in your life. Your body is the temple of God's spirit, and for us to be all that God has called us to be, we have to continuously make conscious efforts to take care of our bodies. As I stated before, research and read about everything. Is there is an area of your life that you are struggling in? Research it. Want to lose weight? Eat healthier? Grow your hair? Get rid of acne? You know what I'm talking about, ladies. All these factors repeatedly plague our minds. Research and gain knowledge about these topics, so you can make healthy choices for yourself and family. I always say every woman should know how to "cook clean." Yes, I know Grandma and Mama may have cooked the best fried chicken, dumplings, and soul food, but there has to be healthier alternatives to some of these family recipes. Ladies, we feed our families most of the time, so let's feed them right. Feed your children home-cooked meals loaded with fruits, vegetables, and dark, leafy greens rather than fast food. Train your children to have a taste for fruits and vegetables as opposed to sugary drinks, cookies, and cakes. There has to be a healthy balance. If they see Mama eating it, guess what? They will eat it.

Ultimately, the self-discipline we practice will influence the rest of our family. It is critical to take your role as a woman in the house seriously. We have work to do for God, and it cannot be accomplished in the capacity that it should be accomplished in if we are sick. Take care of yourself, husband, and children. There are so many healthy initiatives we may take that can keep away obesity, high blood pressure, high cholesterol, cancer, diabetes and other chronic illnesses. These illnesses have become a growing threat to our society. There are many diseases people may bring on themselves simply because of a lack of discipline in their diet or even worse, a lack of knowledge. Begin to train your body to eat a diet rich in vegetables and fruit. You will see tremendous benefits. You cannot keep feeding your body everything it craves; you have to discipline and feed it the proper nutrients for it to function. Food should fuel you for your daily activities.

At some point, you must begin to discipline your flesh and exercise self-control. It goes further than practicing self-control in abstaining from fornication or other sins. We must practice self-control in our eating habits as well. We only receive one body in this lifetime, and it is up to us whether to take care of it. So I encourage you today to take control of your health. Make the decision to eat healthier daily, and you won't have to diet. If you regularly eat what you are supposed to, there is no need for a diet unless you are trying to accomplish weight goals or have other issues. Not only will you have more energy, you will feel great from the inside when you begin to take control over your health.

As with any new health routine, get a doctor's opinion before starting anything. Remember to always do your own research, and read about everything before investing your hard-earned money into it. Knowledge is essential and will empower you to live a healthier life. Ready? Set? Go!

August Goals/Challenges

1) Buy a cookbook that promotes healthy foods (recipes rich in vegetables and fruit). Cook a new dish once a week for your family.

2) If you haven't already, schedule an appointment with your physician. Check your blood pressure, weight, and cholesterol numbers. Talk with your doctor about any healthy choices that need to be made in your life.

3) Write down health-related goals you want to accomplish (for example, going to the gym, drinking more water, eliminating unhealthy snacks). What do you need to give up? What do you need to add?

4) Do one thing this month that you have never done before. Visit an art museum, volunteer at a local shelter, try a new restaurant or new food, and so on. Begin to broaden your horizons about the endless possibilities life has to offer. Open your mind to something new.

Scriptural References

Week 1: "How long, O simple ones, will you love being simple? How long will scoffers delight in their scoffing and fools hate knowledge? (Proverbs 1:22 ESV).

- What does it mean to be *simple*?

- How does this verse describe someone who hates knowledge? Define that term.

- Ask God to show you any areas in your life where you may have turned away from any of his truths. Record what He places on your heart.

- Ask God for knowledge and wisdom over every area of your life.

Week 2: "Therefore, I urge you, brothers, in view of God's mercy, to offer your bodies as living sacrifices, holy and pleasing to God—this is your spiritual act of worship" (Romans 12:1 NIV).

- What is your true and proper worship? Does God want you to treat your body badly?

  _____
  _____
  _____

- What does it mean for you to offer your body as a living sacrifice?

  _____
  _____
  _____

- How can you please God with your body and actions? How can you displease God with your body?

  _____
  _____
  _____
  _____

- The word *offer* indicates God is giving His children a choice on whether to properly live for Him. Why do you believe God gives us such free will concerning our bodies?

  _____
  _____
  _____
  _____

Week 3: "An intelligent heart acquires knowledge, and the ear of the wise seeks knowledge." (Proverbs 18:15 ESV)

Woman, I Am Devotional

- If you acquire knowledge, how does the Bible describe you? Define these two terms.

- Why is it important to acquire knowledge? What if we walked around with a lack of knowledge? Read also Hosea 4:6. What does God say about lacking knowledge?

- How does this Scripture apply to your life? What do you take from it?

- What do you think it means to have an intelligent heart?

Week 4: "I have been crucified with Christ and I no longer live, but Christ lives in me. The life I live in the body, I live by faith in the Son of God, who loved me and gave himself for me" (Galatians 2:20 NIV).

- What habits, behaviors, and mind-sets do you need to crucify today so that Christ can manifest His great power within you? If there are any areas you are struggling with, ask the Holy Spirit for wisdom and knowledge on how to overcome these areas and achieve victory.

    _____
    _____
    _____
    _____
    _____

- According to the above Scripture, how should you live? Why is this important? Now that you have this knowledge, how does it change your perspective about who you are?

    _____
    _____
    _____
    _____
    _____

- Meditate on and write down 2 Corinthians 5:17. How can you apply this Scripture in your life?

    _____
    _____
    _____
    _____
    _____

- If Christ dwells inside you, you have the power and ability to overcome any obstacle in life and to fulfill your purpose. What cares/worries/burdens do you need to release to God today?

Prayer

Father, I desire to be the healthy woman You want me to be. With so many obligations, show me how to be well-balanced. Above all else, help me exercise enough self-control in my life so that I make healthy decisions for myself daily. Father, I ask You to give me strength and restore my determination to exercise and eat healthfully. Help me to train and discipline my flesh so that I will possess the energy, time, and perseverance needed to fulfill my purpose. Help me to honor You every day in my body and to keep my feet from evil and temptation. I give my body as a living sacrifice to you. Jesus paid the price for me. He paid a gruesome price so that I could be reconciled to you. How wonderful is it to know that you love me with such an everlasting love.

Lord, teach me wisdom, knowledge and understanding. As I read my Bible, help me to apply its principles to my life. Help me to be a doer of the word of God. I relinquish control of my life and submit and yield to you today. I know there are areas that I need major help in. I'm tired of trying to control them. I need your power to transform me. Thank you for being my peace of mind and strength. As I grow in knowledge, I will continually give you all the glory, honor and praise. You deserve all of me. In Jesus' name I pray. Amen.

September

The Praying Woman

It was a bright and sunny Saturday afternoon at West Haven Beach in Connecticut. The members of Woman, I Am Incorporated gathered for our monthly meeting, and I posed a question to them: "How do/did you get to know your significant other, and how often do you communicate with them?" Many of the girls replied how they would talk, text, call, and spend time with that person.

This is the attitude we need to bring to our relationship with God. We need to talk and spend time with Him daily. Cultivate a relationship with God. Get rid of religion. God wants to lead and guide you every moment of your life. He has so much to share with you! It is critical to keep open communication with Him every day. If you are happy, pray. If you are mad, angry, disappointed, discouraged—still pray. God has extraordinary plans for your life, but how can you know if you don't communicate with Him? When I wake up in the morning, I constantly remind myself I have a daily meeting with God that I can't afford to miss. If I miss it, I've missed out on vital information for my life. Prayer is essential, valuable, and precious. Cultivate that relationship with God daily, and never allow anything to get in between it. The joy you are looking for—that inner peace, happiness, strength, guidance, direction, and love—are all unlocked through prayer. When you pray, something is happening in the spiritual realm.

We live in two realms—the spiritual and the natural. There is a constant battle between these realms. Your spirit wants and yearns to please God, but your flesh is weak. Put no confidence in the flesh, because it will lead you astray. Your flesh wants to do what is contrary to your spirit and vice versa. Spending time with God, fasting, praying, and living a consecrated life helps keep your flesh under subjection.

Let's be real. If you allow your thoughts to run rampant, it will eventually lead to out-of-control behavior. Your behavior follows your thoughts. The Holy Spirit that dwells on the inside will exercise its fruit of self-control to keep us in line with God's purpose for our lives. You cannot afford to live out of control. So we must guard our hearts and minds with all diligence. I guarantee that as you spend daily time with God, your appetite for worldly desires will fade, and there will be a yearning for more of God. There is no way you can diligently seek God and not be changed. If you stay in the face of Him, such a magnificent light will shine through you.

Why Pray?

Prayer is simple communication with God. Prayer is our lifeline to God. We must pray because it is so essential in developing a healthy spiritual life. The Enemy comes to work against your emotions so you won't feel like praying. When you find yourself easily discouraged, irritated, overwhelmed, burned out, fatigued, and stressed about life's circumstances, these are key signs you haven't been spending enough time with God. He refreshes you and builds up your inner spirit. Just as proper nutrients and exercise are important to keeping your body healthy, so is spending time with God. If you feed your spirit garbage, garbage will flow out of you. Whatever you feed into your body, comes right back out.

If you ever want to really know people, listen to their conversations. Listen to what they talk about. Reflect on your own conversations. What has come out of your mouth lately? Out of the abundance of the heart, the mouth speaks (Matthew 12:34). Whatever is inside your heart will come out of your mouth. So if your heart is full of God's love, love will flow out of you.

I have listed some tips to help you in your prayer time. This is not a commanded list to follow. Rather, it is an aid to help you get the best out of your alone time with God. Jesus Christ is our ultimate example and perfect role model. He often went to solitary places to hear from his heavenly Father. We must always rejoice in Christ's redemptive work on the cross. It is because of His ultimate sacrifice that we are justified and made righteous in the sight of God. You have an opportunity to commune with your heavenly Father because of Christ. You were worth dying for. Let's never take that for granted.

How to Spend Time with God

Find a quiet space

- Give God praise and worship. Take some time to quiet your mind.

Bring a notebook and Bible

- As God begins to speak to your heart, write down what He says. Write down any questions you have for God. Bring those up to Him.

Confession/Repentance

- What is hidden on the inside? Anything you need to confess?
  - Examine yourself and what is in your heart.
  - Repent of your sins daily. Ask the Holy Spirit to show you any area of your life that needs work.

Petition

- What do you need from God?
- When you ask, ask in Jesus' name, in faith, with thanksgiving, and without worry.

Listen

- If you sit still long enough in His presence, God will talk back to you.
- Give God a chance to pour back into you. Listen to Him.

September Goal/Challenge

—I challenge you to choose one person to pray for this entire month. Set aside a particular time in the day that you will pray to God for this person's well-being, health, spiritual walk, and any needs or desires. Allow the Holy Spirit to lead and guide you.

Scriptural References

Week 1: "Therefore confess your sins to each other and pray for each other so that you may be healed. The prayer of a righteous man is powerful and effective" (James 5:16 NIV).

- Do you have any trustworthy friends, leaders, and/or family you can confess your sins to and who will lift you up in prayer? List them. If not, ask God to bring them into your life.

  _____
  _____
  _____

- If you are righteous, what kind of prayers do you possess?

  _____
  _____

- Why should you confess your sins to each other and pray for each other?

  _____
  _____
  _____
  _____
  _____

- Read 1 Timothy 2:1. Do your prayers constantly revolve around your personal needs and wants, or do you pray for others as well?

  _____
  _____
  _____
  _____
  _____
  _____
  _____
  _____

Week 2: "If you believe, you will receive whatever you ask for in prayer" (Matthew 21:22 NIV).

- Why must you believe when you pray?

  _____
  _____
  _____
  _____

- How will you receive what you ask for in prayer? What happens if you pray about a situation, but doubt?

  _____
  _____
  _____
  _____

- Read Mark 11:24.
- Read John 14:13–14.

Week 3: "If you remain in me and my words remain in you, ask whatever you wish, and it will be given you" (John 15:7 NIV).

- Who do you need to remain in? What desires do you have that need to be released in prayer?

  _____
  _____
  _____
  _____

- How do Christ's words remain in you? Are you diligently studying scripture?

- What promise is given to those who remain in Christ and His words remain in them?

- Read and write out Psalm 119:11. How does this Scripture apply to your life?

Week 4: "In my anguish I cried to the lord, and he answered by setting me free. The Lord is with me; I will not be afraid. What can man do to me?" (Psalm 118:5–6 NIV).

- Have you ever been hard-pressed or distressed about a circumstance? What did the author of this psalm do when faced with difficulties? What have you done in the past when faced with difficult circumstances? I challenge you to pray first every time you come against trials and tribulations.

- Who is with you? What did the author have to do before the Lord answered and set him free?

  _____
  _____
  _____

- Memorize the above Scripture for the week until you can say it verbatim.
- How can you begin and continue to trust the Lord and take refuge in Him?

  _____
  _____
  _____
  _____
  _____
  _____
  _____
  _____
  _____
  _____
  _____
  _____
  _____
  _____
  _____
  _____
  _____
  _____
  _____
  _____

Reflection Questions

1) Do you exhibit any form of doubt when you pray to God?

2) Is God your last resort when you are in need, or do you immediately leave your cares and worries at His feet daily?

3) Are you spending daily prayer time with God or rushing throughout your day? How can you slow down and make God a priority?

4) Are you praying before making decisions? If so – do you wait for an answer from God or do what you want to do?

Prayer

Father, in the name of Jesus, I ask that you give me a desire for prayer, praise, and worship. I ask that You speak to my heart day and night, so I may train my ears to hear Your voice. I ask that You remove all burdens of fear from me and replace it with the fire of the Lord. I ask for holy boldness in these last and evil days, so I may proclaim Your glory in all the earth. Help me mature in my walk with You and to reach greater heights, dimensions, and realms in my prayer time.

Open the eyes of my understanding, and take all blinders off my eyes. Holy Spirit, teach me to be persistent in prayer. Help me to obey the voice of God as He gives me daily direction in my life. Lord, forgive me for all of the times when I have dismissed your guidance. Forgive me for all of the times when I started my day without you. Forgive me of my sins. As I go throughout this day, may you quiet my soul so that I may hear clearly from you concerning my life. In Jesus name I pray. Amen.

October
The Wise vs. Foolish Woman

Why Do I Need Wisdom?

Proverbs 1:7 says the fear of the Lord is the beginning of wisdom, but fools despise wisdom and discipline. What does it mean to fear the Lord? You have to respect, honor, and revere God. God wants you to respect Him. Do you honor God today? Does your life honor God today? Do your thoughts and actions honor God today?

According to the Bible, you're a foolish woman if you despise the teaching of God. A foolish woman despises God's wisdom and discipline. Has God been tugging at your heart, trying to get your attention about a situation? What has been your response? I pray you make every necessary step toward becoming a wise woman. How long do you have to go around the same mountain, doing the same thing, until you realize your way doesn't produce the most effective results? Only God's way works.

What Is Wisdom?

The book of Proverbs is often referred to as the wisdom chapter in the Bible. Ultimately, fearing the Lord attains wisdom. You should have such an awe, honor, and reverence toward him, and live a sacrificial life that is a pleasing aroma in His nostrils. Solid wisdom is built on biblical foundations and principles. The Word of God is all you need to stand on. It is powerful and transmits truth.

> For the word of God is living and active. Sharper than any double-edged sword, it penetrates even to dividing soul and spirit, joints and marrow; it judges the thoughts and attitudes of the heart. Nothing in all creation is hidden from God's sight. Everything is uncovered and laid bare before the eyes of him to whom we must give account. (Hebrews 4:12–13 NIV)

Whenever faced with any circumstance in your life, line it up with the Word of God. Go to your Bible, and read what His Word says about it. Then, make a decision based on His guidance. It is so much easier to follow instructions from a book that will never change. The Bible is God's Word, and whatever He says stands the test of time. His words are eternal. You can trust your entire life in the hands of God. He is so gentle and soothing, He will never leave you, He loves you with an everlasting love, and His eyes are always on you, watching. Let's make Him proud in all that we do and all that we are as women.

According to the *Merriam-Webster's Dictionary*, "wisdom" is defined as having intelligence and knowledge.[7] God wants you to display wisdom in every area of your life. It is not God's will for you to live in constant confusion and foolishness. It is critical to learn how to make sound and wise choices as a woman. Wisdom can be

---

[7] "Wisdom." *Webster's New Basic Dictionary & Thesaurus*. 2010. Print.

exercised in finances, relationships, marriage, motherhood, business, jobs—over every area of your life. The book of Proverbs is a great place to start. There are thirty-one proverbs, so read a proverb a day for the month. Reading and studying the Word of God adds life to every dead area. It will refresh and soothe you. The Bible is a magnificent book that accurately depicts the standards we ought to live by. You are a beautiful woman of God.

Sure, we all make mistakes and have had shortcomings, but the first step in making a wise decision is recognizing you aren't who you used to be, and you are not defined by your mistakes. The past is the past. Let it go, and stop letting it hinder your progress. Accept Jesus Christ as your personal savior, and I guarantee your life will never be the same. Only the power of God is able to completely transform you.

How to Apply Wisdom to Your Life

—Accept His words (Proverbs 2:1, author's paraphrase).

—Open your ear to wisdom, and apply your heart to understanding (Proverbs 2:2, author's paraphrase).

—Call out for insight, and cry out for understanding (Proverbs 2:3, author's paraphrase).

—Look and search for it as for silver and hidden treasure (Proverbs 2:4, author's paraphrase).

What Does Wisdom Do for Your Life?

—It enters your heart (Proverbs 2:10, author's paraphrase).

—Wisdom saves you from the ways of wicked and evil people (Proverbs 2:12, author's paraphrase).

—Wisdom saves you from the adulteress (Proverbs 2:16, author's paraphrase).

—Wisdom causes you to walk in the way of good people and keep to the paths of the righteous (Proverbs 2:20, author's paraphrase).

—Wisdom prolongs your life by many years and brings you prosperity (Proverbs 3:2, author's paraphrase).

—Wisdom brings health and nourishment to your body and bones (Proverbs 3:8, author's paraphrase).

—Wisdom protects you and watches over you (Proverbs 4:6, author's paraphrase).

—You will live (Proverbs 7:2, author's paraphrase).

—The Lord bestows wealth on those who love Him and makes their treasures full (Proverbs 8:21, author's paraphrase).

What Happens if you Reject Wisdom, Follow Foolish and Rebellious Paths, and Follow the Ways of Evil People?

—It takes away your life (Proverbs 1:19, author's paraphrase).

—God will laugh at your disaster/ruin (Proverbs 1:24–32, author's paraphrase).

—You will be cut off (Proverbs 2:22, author's paraphrase).

—You will walk in darkness (Proverbs 4:19, author's paraphrase).

—You will be ensnared (Proverbs 5:22, author's paraphrase).

Benefits of a Wise Woman

The wise woman is teachable. She receives and loves instruction. This woman grows in wisdom. She fears the Lord. She hates what is evil and false. She shuns evil and does what is right. The wise woman speaks the truth in love, is humble and not proud, is self-controlled, has a calm spirit, is slow to anger, and is forgiving and patient. She is concerned about the goodwill/peace of others. She forgives those who wrong her and is not vindictive. The wise woman trusts in the Lord. She chooses the Lord's way/wisdom and submits to the Lord's discipline. She respects her parents and seeks to bring them both honor and joy. She is not boastful, argumentative, nor a gossiper. She doesn't reveal secrets or slanders. Her mind is governed by true, authentic and positive thoughts. She avoids strife, has compassion for humans and animals, and is diligent, faithful, generous, and honest.

The wise woman is a noble wife and lives with a gentle and peaceful spirit.

You may look at this list and think, *Wow, it is impossible for any woman to attain all these attributes.* Don't worry, if you strive for godliness and righteousness daily, everything mentioned in that list will fall into divine alignment. It is the power of the Holy Spirit working through you that corrects every area of your life. True conviction from the Holy Spirit leads you and guides you to all truth. You may not have every single attribute listed, but with the help of the Holy Spirit, you should continually strive, without fear or hesitation, to be the woman God has called you to be.

As you begin to live for God, your appetite begins to change, and you will not desire the things you used to want. Your spirit and mind will begin to transform, and your life will begin to line up with the Word of God. When you live in darkness, you can't imagine attaining those attributes. But as you step into the light, your life will be changed.

A Foolish Woman

Foolishness is literally the opposite of wisdom. What would it profit you to walk around without any sense, judgment, or discretion? What does God say about fools and foolish behavior? Let's take a look.

> He who trusts in himself is a fool, but he who walks in wisdom is kept safe. (Proverbs 28:26 NIV)

Are you trusting merely in yourself, or have you put your life in the hands of God, who knows all things?

> A fool finds no pleasure in understanding but delights in airing his own opinions. (Proverbs 18:2 NIV)

Do you have a desire to gain understanding about God, your life, your future, and your destiny? Or have you told yourself, "I've got this all figured out." A foolish woman doesn't delight in understanding and falsely believes she has it all figured out. God is the Creator of all eternity. He knows your coming in and going out. If there is anyone who can lead you in the right path, it is Him.

> A fool's lips bring him strife, and his mouth invites a beating. (Proverbs 18:6 NIV)

Has your mouth ever gotten you into trouble? Watch your words. You can invite negative forces into your life through negative, spiteful, and idle conversation.

> A fool's mouth is his undoing, and his lips are a snare to his soul. (Proverbs 18:7 NIV)

Have you brought destruction on yourself by your lips? Has your soul been ensnared by your spoken words? A foolish woman is quick to speak in anger and babbles on while never giving thought to what comes out of her mouth. Guard your mouth!

> Folly delights a man who lacks judgment, but a man of understanding keeps a straight course. (Proverbs 15:21 NIV)

> A wise man fears the Lord and shuns evil, but a fool is hotheaded and reckless. (Proverbs 14:16 NIV)

Reckless behavior is destructive. Reckless speech is even more damaging. A foolish woman disregards good and pursues evil with her words. Your words are supposed to be like honey dripping from your lips—encouraging, soothing, and edifying everyone around you.

> The fool folds his hands and ruins himself. (Ecclesiastes 4:5 NIV)

A lazy woman ruins herself.

> Wise men store up knowledge, but the mouth of a fool invites ruin. (Proverbs 10:14 NIV)

Once again, we witness how your mouth can invite ruin and destruction in your life. A wise woman stores knowledge and prospers in all she does. Yet a foolish woman invites ruin. For example, when you invite someone to your house, you willingly welcome in him or her. They show up at the door, you open the door, and invite them in. Let's think about this analogy with our own mouths and words. Similarly, you can invite negativity into your life by opening the door to damaging and harmful ruin through your words. The choice is yours.

October Goal/Challenge

This month, focus on the book of Proverbs, because it was designed to give believers wisdom and discipline, to understand words of insight, to acquire a disciplined and prudent life, to do what is just and fair, to give prudence to the simple, and knowledge and discretion to the young (Proverbs 1:1–4 NIV).

Scriptural References

Read one proverb a day and record below the Scriptures that spoke the most to your heart.

Reflection Questions

1) Reflect and record any areas of your life you may have been foolish in or need to change or improve. Be honest with yourself, and seek God for a renewed heart. That is the first step to change.

Relationships

—Has there been continuous nonsense that you have put up with while in a relationship?

—Have you manipulated your mate in any manner? Why?

—Are you in a relationship God has not ordained for you?

—Do you put your boyfriend/husband above God (idolatry)?

—Do you seek to please your mate over God?

—Is your mate pushing you toward God or away from Him?

—Have you compromised your standards?

—Do you respect and listen to your parents?

—Do you value the people God has blessed you with in your life? Do you show them love?

—Do you strive for peace or strife?

Money

—Do you spend carelessly, without any consideration of bills?

—Do you spend all that you have and never save?

—Do you try to keep up with the Joneses?

—Do you live above your means to impress others?

—Do you pay your bills on time?

—Are you responsible with your checking and/or savings account?

Decision Making

—Do you give thought to your steps?

—Do you seek the advice of your friends before asking God what He thinks about the matter?

—Are you gullible?

—Do you make rational decisions and think for yourself, or do you consult everyone else before you come to a conclusion?

—Are you emotionally driven and make decisions based on how you feel at the moment?

—Are you growing in wisdom?

—Do you have a calm spirit, or are you easily angered?

—Do you think before you speak?

Character

—Are you proud, prideful, or hasty?

—Are you teachable?

—Are you growing in wisdom?

—Are you trustworthy?

—Do you gossip?

—Are you always complaining?

—Are you double-minded?

—Do you stand up for what is right, just, and fair?

—Are you forgiving?

—Are you vindictive?

2) What necessary changes need to be implemented for you to walk in wisdom? Where do you need to start?

Read and pray according to Psalm 119:29–40. What is the author asking the Lord for?

_____
_____
_____
_____
_____

What is the author asking God to teach him?

_____
_____
_____
_____

What is the author asking God to turn his eyes from? Why do you think he is asking God this?

_____
_____
_____
_____
_____
_____
_____

Prayer

Father, I desire wisdom over every area of my life. You said in James 1:5 that if any man lacks wisdom, he should ask of God, who gives to all without finding fault. Therefore, I ask according to Your Word for wisdom. There are unanswered questions and areas of my life that need clarity. I desire to be a wise woman over a foolish woman, but I need Your help. You said You will never leave me and are with me always—even until the end of time. I thank You for pouring Your wisdom unto me. May I grow in wisdom each and every day and live a life that is pleasing to Your sight. In Jesus' name I pray, Amen.

November

Insecurity, Fear, and Rejection: Those Hidden Darts

A mirror was designed to reflect whatever image was placed before it. When you look in the mirror, what do you see? Do your pimples, eyebrows, or other facial features catch your attention first? Or do you look deeper than that? Do you look in the mirror and see a God-fearing woman, poised with strength, dignity, and beauty who is laughing without fear of the future? Sure, we all have those days where we may not feel "up to par," but is image merely what you measure your beauty by? Isn't beauty deeper than that? Doesn't true beauty reflect the soul of a woman—her reverence for the Lord? How do you define beauty? What makes you beautiful?

Insecurity stems from a lack of confidence, a negative perspective of self-identity, and a lack of healthy self-esteem. Insecurity feeds and thrives on incapability. You look at what others have over what God has blessed you with. Insecurity makes you feel like you are inadequate to performing the tasks at hand. If the Enemy can keep your focus on who you aren't, you will never become the woman God intended you to be. You must shift your focus back to God.

There is an underlying root to the spirit of insecurity. You weren't born insecure, but something happened to invite that negative force into your life. Maybe you were teased as a young girl. Perhaps you grew up in a broken home or have never felt encouragement or love from your parents or peers. Those are all circumstances and opportunities for the Enemy to birth fear, insecurity, and low self-esteem within you. Then, as time goes on, other negative factors feed that insecurity, allowing that negative spirit to grow and magnify. Before you know it, you walk around with your head down, unable to see the beautiful woman God has created you to be. It is all detrimental cycles, ones the Enemy uses to keep women in bondage. Cycles the Enemy uses to blind, deceive, and manipulate women into thinking they don't deserve the best of everything in their lives.

Evaluate your personal relationships. How you allow people to treat you shows how valuable you believe you are. If you allow people to walk all over you could mean you may not believe you are worthy to be treated with dignity and respect. My precious sister, please understand your value and worth. You are the daughter of the most High God and the apple of His eyes. You are precious and worth loving. Whatever the case may be, settle it in your heart today that you are loved so deeply by your heavenly Father. Christ is able to deliver you from insecurity.

Wherever you find insecurity, fear and rejection are its counterparts. Rejection is like a hole. You don't feel worthy enough. When you are rejected for any reason, you go out and try to fill that hole and void to feel complete. Everyone wants to feel complete. Everyone wants to feel wanted and needed. Fornication, money, drugs, drinking, partying, detrimental relationships, and other "void fillers" are temporary. It may feel good for the moment, but ultimately, the void is still there once those fillers cease. Rejection will cause you to act out of character. It can bring ungodly behavior out of you, behavior you didn't even know you were capable of exhibiting. Rejection turns to pity parties, which leads to sorrow, depression, oppression, stress, anxiety, and many other factors.

As the Enemy feeds on your rejection, he adds in fear. Now you are timid and frightened, unable to maximize your potential because of fear. Fear is a poisonous bondage that entangles helpless victims every day. Perfect love casts out all fear. Fear and love cannot dwell in the same temple. If the Enemy can keep you fearful, you won't step out on your purpose, you won't fulfill your destiny, you'll never start that business, you'll never apply for that school, you'll never venture into that dream job. All because you listened to the lies seeping out of the mouth of the Father of Lies. Every believer has power and authority through Jesus Christ over the Enemy and his satanic forces. Never think that insecurity has overcome you and there is no way out. That is what the Enemy wants you to believe. But you are more than a conqueror and able to stand against the wiles of the Devil. God is with you wherever you go, therefore do not be afraid.

A life of insecurity, low self-esteem, fear, and rejection is not for the woman God intended you to be. He wants you to be set free and delivered from those bondages. It is the anointing of Christ that is able to destroy every yoke of bondage of your life, loosen the shackles of insecurity, and set your feet on solid ground. You have to believe in your heart that God has greater for you. You have to see it in your mind before it manifests. See yourself walking boldly, confidently, with your head held high. See yourself living the life of your dreams and fulfilling your purpose. It is possible. You are that woman God has called into the forefront to proclaim His glory in all the land. You are that world changer. You are that businesswoman. You are that scholar. You are that prayer warrior and intercessor. What are you afraid of? What can touch you when you have the power of God inside of you? You are never alone. God the Father, Jesus, the Holy Spirit, and a host of angels encamp around you and are with you. What can others do to you?

Someone is waiting for your kind words and gentle hands to help him or her. Remember we are helpers and all have assignments. Don't allow fear, rejection, or insecurity to stop you from fulfilling your tasks. Ultimately, we all have to give an account to God for everything we have done—and haven't done. You want to be confident when you stand before Him, knowing that you used every gift and talent He placed inside you to help humanity, advance His kingdom, and bring Him glory.

You must make up your mind that you believe God is who He says He is and that come hell or high water, you will fulfill your purpose. Overcoming insecurity takes time. I recommend daily feeding your inner spirit with the Word of God. When you feed your spirit through praise, prayer, worship, and the Word of God, you feed your spirit the necessary nutrients needed for it to function and grow properly. Your inner woman needs to be nurtured as well. Your mind must be renewed. Are you in need of a mind makeover? You are transformed by the renewing of your mind by washing it over with the Word of God. Think of the Word of God as water that washes away all the impurities and toxins you have accumulated from the world. As you read the Word, it begins to cleanse you and transmits truth to your soul. You begin to see yourself in a different light. You begin to see yourself the way God sees you. You begin to drown out the world's voice and tune into God's voice. His is the only voice that matters because He is your Creator. You can do whatever you put your mind to. You are equipped to accomplish every goal and desire. Remember that someone needs you.

November Challenges

1) Write down any fears you have on a piece of paper. Pray over this list, and ask God to help you overcome your fears. I challenge you to try something this month that you have been holding back on because of fear (starting a business, writing a book, going to school, applying for a certain job, and so on).

Scriptural References

Week 1: "There is no fear in love. But perfect love drives out fear, because fear has to do with punishment. The one who fears is not made perfect in love" (1 John 4:18 NIV).

- What casts out all fear? If you are walking in fear, what hasn't been perfected in your life yet? What steps can you take to perfect love in your life?

  _____
  _____
  _____
  _____

- List another Scripture that references overcoming fear. Meditate on this Scripture. Speak it over your life.

  _____
  _____
  _____

- The next time fear tries to rise inside of you, what can you do to counteract that feeling?

  _____
  _____
  _____
  _____
  _____
  _____

Woman, I Am Devotional

Week 2: "No one will be able to stand up against you all the days of your life. As I was with Moses, so I will be with you; I will never leave you nor forsake you" (Joshua 1:5 NIV).

- What assurance does God give every believer? Do you believe God?

- What was going on during this time for God to reassure Joshua of His presence and constant comfort? Read surrounding passages.

- How can you take steps toward trusting God with your whole heart and letting go of all fear?

- Read the story of Moses (Exodus 2-Deuteronomy 34). How did God use Moses? What obstacles did Moses come against while fulfilling his purpose? How did Moses respond when trials and tribulations arose? In what ways did Moses trust God? What did trusting God result in for Moses?

_____
_____
_____
_____
_____
_____
_____
_____
_____
_____
_____
_____
_____
_____
_____
_____
_____
_____
_____
_____

Week 3: "But the Lord said to Samuel, 'Do not consider his appearance or his height, for I have rejected him.' The Lord does not look at the things man look at. Man looks at the outward appearance, but the Lord looks at the heart" (1 Samuel 16:7 NIV).

- What makes the Lord different from people?

  _____
  _____
  _____

- Even if you may have been rejected or abandoned, what does God look at? How does this comfort you?

  _____
  _____
  _____
  _____

- Why does God place emphasis on looking at the heart? What is so essential about someone's heart?

  _____
  _____
  _____
  _____
  _____

- How does this Scripture apply to your life? How can this Scripture comfort you?

  _____
  _____
  _____
  _____

Week 4: "For God gave us a spirit not of fear but of power and love and self control" (2 Timothy 1:7 ESV).

- According to this Scripture, what has God given you? Do you accept these words?

- Feeling timid or fearful? Write down this scripture and put your name in it. Repeat this confession daily.

- How does this scripture make you feel? Are you comforted?

- For another reference of your uniqueness, read Luke 12:7.

Reflection Questions

1) If you are dealing with fear, rejection or insecurity, ask the Holy Spirit to show you how it entered into your life. Decide today that you will not be a victim anymore! Get to the root and pluck it out from your life.

2) Do you truly believe God wants the best for your life? Continue to speak positive affirmations over your life. Hang positive scriptures and quotes around your house. Remind yourself of who you are.

Prayer

Lord, today I accept myself the way You accept me. No one can love me the way You do. In my darkest moments, You were there for me and continue to be there for me. Forgive me for not accepting myself as the beautiful creation You designed me to be. Teach me through Your Word, and teach me through the Holy Spirit how to love myself and accept Jesus' redemptive work on the cross. I am fearfully and wonderfully made, without any flaws. May I constantly encourage and strengthen myself in and through You. May I never compare myself to other women but continually seek my identity, which is found in Christ Jesus alone. Thank You for my future and for what is to come. I praise You in advance for the awesome plans that were strategically planned before the foundation of this world. Keep my eyes focused on You at all times, and let me not stray from You. In Jesus' name, I pray. Amen.

*To conclude the year, December's devotional will provide further encouragement for you to step out on your dreams.

December

The Bold Woman: Stepping out on a Vision

I am so glad you stuck through with this devotional, and I hope you have been learning more about yourself through this book. Let me make this clear: you have a vision/dream inside you. You may not be aware of it or recognize it, but it is there. God has placed visions, dreams, and aspirations in every person, but it is up to us to see Him for who He is. He will open your eyes to the vision (Jeremiah 29:11).

Any vision you want to manifest is going to take much prayer, time, patience, self-control, organization, the leading of the Holy Spirit, and wisdom. Don't fret, God is with you. You may not know all the answers quite yet, but God will reveal those things in due time. The more you walk in obedience and faith, the more information God will reveal to you. I have learned so much about myself when I decided to launch Woman, I Am Incorporated. At first I didn't think I could do it, because I was looking at everything I didn't have. But the Lord began to deal with me and confirmed that if He provides a vision, He will provide provision. I began to ponder on whom I knew, what contacts and community resources were available. I researched support groups and sat down with knowledgeable sources with wisdom in that field. There are leaders already in the field you are trying to enter. Talk to them about their journeys. Ask them how they got where they are. It will save you a lot of headaches by simply asking questions. Ask as many questions as you need to ask. It is so important to also sit down with your spiritual leaders (pastors, and so) for their sound advice and wisdom. I thank God for my pastors, who have led, corrected, and guided me in the right direction. They see further than you can.

So let's do away with the, "I can't do," and allow God to use you. Stepping out on any vision takes hard work, dedication, and commitment. It will take sacrifices—both financially and in time. But just think about it. You are employed by God to advance the kingdom of God. Whatever vision you have will bring God glory. This is an opportunity for you to share the love of God and reach lost souls through your gifts and talents. Think about all the people who die and go to hell every day. We have the potential to turn them from their wicked ways by pointing them in the right direction. If we could just reach them. If we could just draw them in with love, the same way God drew us in. God will see you through; all you have to do is believe. I encourage you to live the life God ordained for you. People need your help, and it's urgent. Let's all take heed to the assignments set before us, and begin to change the world through God's love. You must be bold. If you struggle with boldness, look up every scripture on being bold and confess it over yourself daily. Following are some principles and tips to help you in making your vision a reality and stepping out boldly.

Principles of Your Purpose

Your gifts and talents work together to fulfill your God-given purpose on earth.

Your Purpose Must Glorify God

At some point in your life, you will come to a crossroad, where you have to choose whether to use your talents for the devil or to advance the kingdom of God. He created you to always worship and glorify Him with everything you do. Apart from Christ, we are nothing. People can literally be categorized as "the walking dead." Christ gives life to you, revives your spirit, and opens your spiritual ears and eyes. Without Christ, your spirit is dead. Feed your spirit the Word of God, prayer, and stay in constant communion /fellowship/ prayer with God. Are you alive in Christ today, or are you spiritually dead? Your body is an instrument. Give God your body as a living sacrifice to Him. That means whatever you set your hands to do must represent God and bring Him delight. We must glorify Him because He is God and deserves it. He loves you so much. Allow your gifts and talents to glorify Him.

Your Purpose Will Serve Humanity

God is in the "people business." It is not His desire for anyone to perish and not have a relationship with Him. You must help someone else. If you are a born-again believer, your Savior, Christ, died for you. He helped you. If we are supposed to live a life that mirrors Christ's, it's a shame and the audacity of some Christians to not give out a helping hand to others. Someone needs your help. Someone is waiting on you to let God use you to help him or her. There are specific people already assigned to you. But guess what? If you want to be disobedient and choose to turn your back to Christ, He will find someone else to do the job. There will always be someone more qualified than you, but you never want God to give your assignments to someone else.

You Must Grow in Your Gifts and Talents

Don't spend and waste unnecessary time doing a million things when you could be exercising and growing in your talent. Stir up your gifts. Cultivate the seed of greatness inside of you. Use what you have first. Become an expert in your field. Study and research. Do whatever you have to do to perfect your gifts.

Your Gifts and Talents Will Make Room for You

God gives you the power to create wealth. Nowhere in the Bible does it say God wants His children poor and begging. God wants you wealthy and prosperous and with the best things in life. Sure, you have to work your way up there, but when you walk in your purpose and exercise your gift, you do not have to chase money or indulge in get-rich-quick schemes. The money will chase after you. People will be scouting for you.

The Bible has principles to teach you how to get wealth. Broke? In debt? Want financial increase? Open your Bible, search the Scriptures to find exactly what your situation is, and put those Scriptures in your mouth. You have what you say. Speak positively, and positive will happen in your life. If you speak negatively and defeated, you will live in defeat. Watch what you say about yourself and to others. Words are powerful and can also be poisonous. I guarantee if you stay in the face of God, be a doer of the Word of God, obey His commandments, walk with Him, and let Him have His way in your life, everything you set your hands to will succeed. He takes care of His children. We are the apples of His eyes. Prosper, my sisters. Live on top of the world. It is ours!

Give!

As you walk in your purpose and the Lord begins to bless you financially, please always remember where you came from and give back. Never be stingy and selfish or try to keep everything to yourself. How can the Lord continue to bless you if your hands are always closed? Give, and it will be given unto you. The principles of sowing and reaping apply to every part of your life. Whatever you give comes back to you. If you sow money, money is reaped; if you constantly give away clothes and shoes, clothes and shoes will come back to you. Whatever your hands find to do, do with all diligence and with a spirit of excellence. Remember that God can't bless closed hands, so open your hands to others, just as our humble Savior did.

Be humble, and never exalt yourself. God will do the exalting. You never want pride to slip in, because without God, we are nothing. So all glory goes to Him.

You Are a Visionary

Write down the vision, and make it plain. Begin to map out your long-term and short-term goals. You must first see who you want to be in your mind. What steps do you need to take now in order to reach those future goals? Research. Plan ahead. Stay organized. Break all bad habits of procrastination. Execute.

You Are a Problem Solver

There is a problem in this world with your name written on it. Your purpose is designed to help solve this problem. Ask God what is it that you are assigned to do. You carry the answer to someone's problem in your belly. Let it flow !

Learn What to Say No To

As you walk with God, begin to prioritize. What is eating up your time? What things do you need to say no to? What places do you need to give up going to? What health habits do you need to implement or bad health habits do you need to break? Your time is valuable and precious. Don't be a time waster. Every moment counts, so seize every opportunity to be great. Say no to distractions and use your time wisely.

God Will Guide You

Trust the plan that God has for your life. If you have trust issues, bring them to God. He will not hurt you and only wants what is best for you. We need His help. He already has your entire life planned out. God will bring the necessary financial resources and the right people in your life in order for you to fulfill your purpose. You have to come into alignment with the plans that have already been established.

Sometimes, I sit and wonder what this world would be like if we all were walking and working in our God-ordained purposes. Imagine a reality where we live in such harmony and unity – that God is thoroughly pleased with His creation. How much talent goes to the grave everyday? How many students go home discouraged because of the immense amount of pressure on them to obtain a degree – but their creative abilities are suffocated? We should never eliminate or ignore the creativity that lies on the inside of us. Everyone was born with seeds of greatness – and you came to this earth equipped. Some of the most beautiful skyscrapers and buildings were first a thought in the mind of God and strategically placed in the heart of creation. Makes you wonder – can we even fathom or measure the capacity of the Lord's creativity? He is just that great, His works are just that marvelous and how humbling and beautiful is it to know that He delights in downloading these visions into the hearts of His children! All you may need is support and encouragement that would empower you to look deeper. Everything you need, you already have. Dig deeper into the depths of your soul and realize the power and potential inside of you. You don't have to look to your friends and loved ones for assurance or confirmation of who you are. God already validated and appointed you before you were in your mother's womb. Stop looking for other people to validate or qualify you for an inheritance that was already paid for by Christ. Allow God to use you in a mighty way and guide you into destiny– the world needs it.

How Do I Get My Vision Off the Ground?

1) Every vision may not require a business plan, but you do want some type of organized and clearly written blueprint.

2) You must have a prayer life. Simple but often overlooked. Let's make it clear that this is God's vision, and He called and trusts you with it! Therefore, let Him guide you on every path to take. Keep open communication with Him so that you aren't easily deceived or manipulated while stepping out. God will grant you the wisdom you need concerning the paths to take and the right people to work with (1 Thessalonians 5:17).

3) Write the vision. Buy a notebook designed specifically for your vision and carry it around with you. You may be inspired anywhere. Write out everything you want to do. What does your vision look like? How will it help others? Who do you need to be on your team? Don't just write once, keep revising (Habakkuk 2:2).

4) Have faith/believe. You must have confidence and faith in yourself and God. He wants to prosper you. This is no time to doubt. Don't be afraid of being successful. God is with you (Mark 9:23).

5) Research your vision. The Internet has tons of information for starting businesses/innovative ideas. Download "business plan" templates, research local companies that provide funding for

businesses, and so on. Take advantage of free workshops in your area. Take time to plan and outline your vision/dream.

6) Don't share everything with everyone. Watch whom you share your ideas with, because someone can take your idea and make it his or her own. Surround yourself with like-minded individuals who genuinely want to see you go higher. God is the one in whom you should always go to for guidance, and ask Him to send you resources. (Genesis 37:5).

Remember to think your way through the vision. Take some quiet time daily to reflect on any goals you set. You already have the dream inside you. Think about what resources you already have. Who do you know? What networking opportunities do you have? Think. Think. Think.

Above all else, please remember we don't come to God so that we can get what we want. Loving God simply for who He is will allow everything else to line up. Christ came so you could have a satisfying life. That means He wants you to be prosperous and successful. However, don't become so stuck on achieving goals that you forget about God. Or worse off, that you don't enjoy your journey. There has to be a healthy balance.

Keep in mind God doesn't reveal the entire picture all at once. It will happen in steps and seasons of your life. Don't become discouraged if you haven't figured out your purpose yet. Seek God through prayer and private time. Ask for wisdom to discern the different seasons. Fellowship with Christ, and read the Word of God daily. God will begin to reveal things to you about your life as you mature in Him. He knows just how much you can handle at a certain time, so as long as you are in the face of God, there will be no regrets.

I don't know what your purpose is. Only God knows because He designed you. Whatever the Lord has called you to do, do it in an excellent and efficient manner, as if you were doing it for God. God equips those who are called. Fear may try to creep up if you feel unworthy for such a responsibility for God. But God said He would never leave you or forsake you. He is right beside you, cheering you on. He has your back. You're His child, and He wants to see the best for you by all means. Therefore, full faith cancels out all fear. Don't let fear hinder you. There are no wimps in the army of the Lord. We are bold soldiers for Christ, standing up for God no matter where we are. Never be ashamed of Him, because He is never ashamed of you.

I used to want to be a news reporter for CNN. That was my dream job as a child, but then as I began to really walk with Christ about a year ago, God began to reveal to me visions that blew my mind. The visions He has given me still use my journalistic gifts and talents but now on a larger scale and for the kingdom of God. Dream bigger than you can ever imagine! The possibilities are endless with God. Have fun with Him. This is your Lord.

Last but not least, always remember to keep praying, no matter what. Never move out on something until you have sought God, and He has given you an answer. Wait on God's perfect timing. God bless.

Everything is possible for one who believes. (Mark 9:23)

Salvation Prayer

Has God tugged at your heart while reading this book? It is never too late to make Jesus Christ your Lord and Savior. Below is a prayer for salvation if you choose to make that step and accept Christ into your heart. Accepting Christ into your life is the best decision you will ever make. A few scriptures to meditate on are ***John 3:16*** and **Romans 10:9-10**.

Prayer:

> Father God in the name of Jesus, I acknowledge myself as a sinner. I need your help. I know you have awesome plans for my life. I ask that you forgive me of my sins and wash me clean of every evil impurity. Lord, I ask you to come into my heart. According to Romans 10:9-10, I confess with my mouth that Jesus is Lord and I believe in my heart that God raised you from the dead. For with my heart I believe and am justified, and with my mouth, I have made confession. Thank you Lord for eternal life with you and thank you Lord for saving me!

About the Author

Chardoneé Wright has sat under the leadership and training of Dr. Mattie A. Darden and Executive Pastor Willa D. Moody of Agape Christian Center for seventeen years. She has held many church leadership roles, including youth leader, minister in training, and reporter for *Agape Advocate,* the church's newsletter. She holds a bachelor's of science degree in journalism and is pursuing a master's of science in global affairs, with a gender specialization in women's studies at New York University.

Referenced Works

1) *The Holy Bible, English Standard Version Global Study Bible*. 2011 ed. Wheaton, Illinois: Crossway, 2011. Print.
2) *The Holy Bible, Zondervan New International Version Study Bible*. 2008 ed. Grand Rapids, Michigan: Zondervan, 2008. Print.
3) *Webster's New Basic Dictionary & Thesaurus*. New York, NY: Minerva, 2010. Print.

Made in the USA
Middletown, DE
05 April 2019